HARTEST: A VILLAGE HISTORY

HARTEST

A Village History

Researched by The Hartest Local History Group

Edited by Clive Paine

Published by
The Hartest Local History Group

First published 1984

ISBN 0 9510180 0 0

Printed in Great Britain by the Lavenham Press Ltd., Lavenham, Suffolk

Contents

Illustrations

Figures

Plates

Foreword

A major watershed in the life of any village is the publication of its first parish history. When such a book is written by local people themselves, the achievement is doubly significant. I have long regarded Hartest as one of the most attractive of Suffolk's villages, and wholeheartedly welcome this proof that it is also a flourishing community concerned about its own character, heritage and future.

It also gives me pleasure that this book results from a successful adult class, sponsored by my department and ably tutored by my friend Clive Paine. I congratulate him and members of the class on unearthing a great deal of local evidence and constructing an enjoyable account of village life. Local history is not a static form of knowledge, but has the priceless advantage of drawing people together in exploration, discussion and communal self-awareness. Because it now knows more about itself, Hartest will never be quite the same again!

David Dymond

3rd December 1984 Stanton, Suffolk

Acknowledgements

We are grateful to the following for permission to use illustrations: Philip Knachel, Deputy Director of the Folger Shakespeare Library, Washington D.C. for manuscript Va.311, 'A Book of Diverse Devices by Thomas Fella of Dunwich', which appears on pages 4, 7, 9, 11, 12, 26, 34, 48 and 78; Amanda Arrowsmith, County Archivist of Suffolk for pages 15, 19, 51, 55, 56, 61, 110, 113, 141 and 142; Mrs. Nancy Weller Poley for page 45; Mrs. P. Ward, churchwarden of Hartest, for page 37; Ernie Pask for pages 80, 82, 93, 100, 106, 109, 111, 114, 127, 128, 131, 132, 134, 136, 138, 140; and Jo Pask for pages 102 and 108.

The following people and organisations have generously made gifts or loans towards the costs of publication: Hartest Community Council; Hartest Parish Council; David Pask, Miss Ivy Pask; Jo Pask; Mrs. Nancy Weller Poley; Sparke's Charity; and Peter Stevens.

Introduction

This publication is the result of a three year linked sessional class in local history, sponsored by the University of Cambridge Board of Extra-Mural Studies. At the instigation of Peter Stevens, who became the class secretary, I began a series of introductory lectures in September 1981. During this first year twenty-six people joined the class, and we are grateful for their financial help and continued interest, which enabled the research group to continue for a further two years.

Our aim was to discover as much as was possible about the major themes of village life in the 17th and 19th centuries. The enthusiasm and achievement of the group can be judged from the following pages.

The members of the first year's class were: Marian and John Aldridge, George Arghyrakis, Ann Bennett, Elizabeth Clark, Joan Dean, Tessa and John English, Jim and Liz Fear, Sue Feather, David Konrath, Jennifer and Michael Laflin, Gilbert Lowes, Richard Weller Poley, David Pask, Ernie Pask, Jo Pask, Nevil Pawsey, Jan Rallings, Martin Raper, Dominic Short, Mabel Smith, Peter Stevens, and Rev. Tom Wright.

The research group, whose names ought to be carved in stone (although not on 'The Stone'!) as a monument to their dedication were: Marian Aldridge, Joan Dean, Liz Fear, Martin Raper and Dominic Short, who worked on the 17th century; Ann Bennet, Wendy Coen, John English, Ian Konrath, Derek McLeod, David Pask and Jo Pask, who worked on the 19th century; and Peter Stevens who drew all the maps.

My personal thanks, as tutor and editor, go to the group for allowing me to help them discover something about the history of their community, and for their friendship and hospitality over numerous cups of coffee, during the past three years.

My thanks are also due to my friends: to David Dymond of Stanton, Resident Tutor in Suffolk for the Extra Mural Board, for his ever helpful advice and encouragement, and for writing the Foreword; to Peter Northeast of Rattlesden, for his generous help, especially on things ecclesiastical; to Sylvia Colman of Euston, for the reconstruction of 'Kings'; to Bernard Abrey of Risby, for his assistance with the agricultural sections; to David Caruth of Gt. Barton, for reading the galleys; and to Joan Dean of Hartest, who undertook the mammoth task of typing the entire text.

Especial thanks must go to my wife Dorothy for her patience and toleration, whilst living through two-hundred years of Hartest history in the last six months.

Clive Paine
12 Hardwick Lane
Bury St. Edmunds

8th December 1984

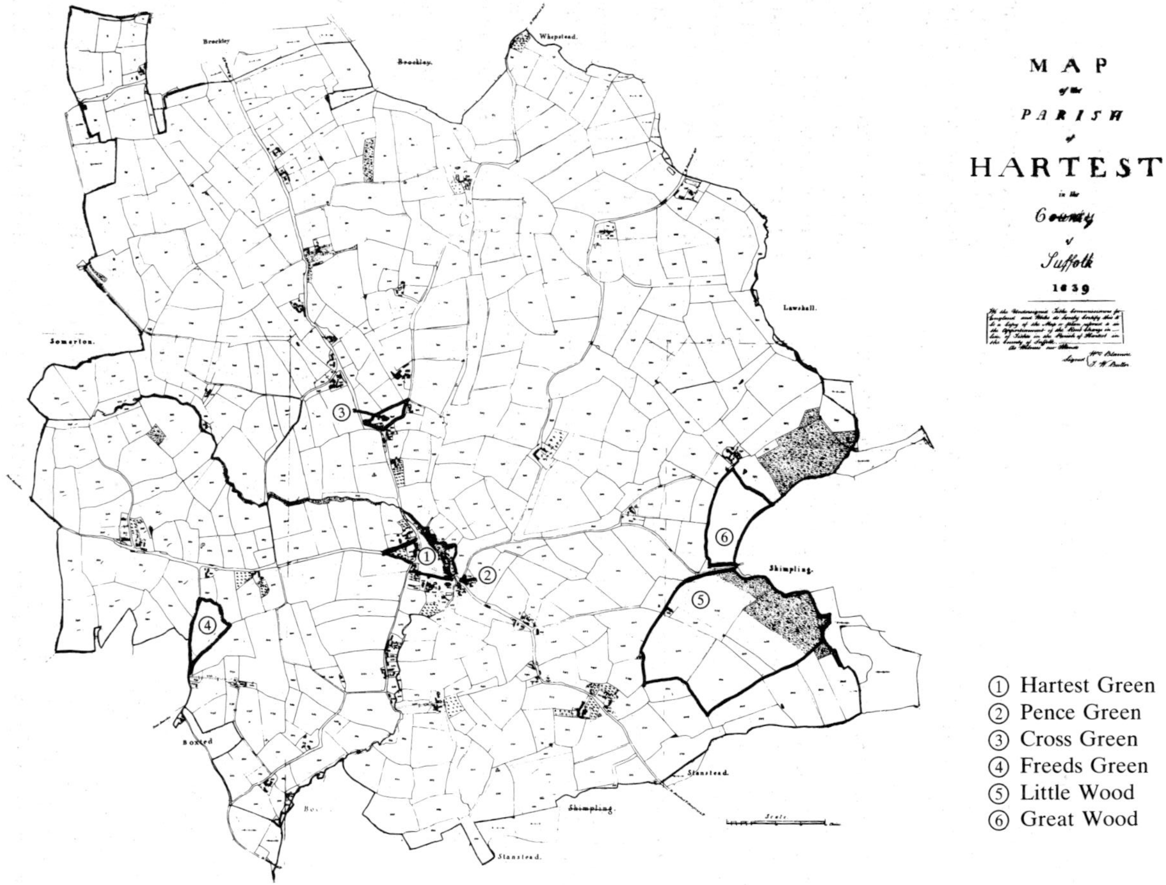

Map 1. The Tithe Map of 1839.

The Settlement

Hartest is situated in the area known as High Suffolk, which is characterised by heavy loam and clay soils, originally covered by woodland and forest.

Indeed the name Hartest is derived from the wooded nature of the landscape. Earlier spellings such as Hertest (c.1050), Herterst (c.1086), Herthyrst (c.1095) and Herthest (1200) contain two elements meaning 'hart' (or stag) and 'wood'. The name Hartest therefore originally meant Harts Wood (1).

Woodland is mentioned in Domesday Book (c.1086), but no area is given or can be inferred. However, a survey of the Abbot of Ely's lands in 1251 gives the area of woodland as 170 acres (2). The two main woods of Hartest were called Great and Little. Manorial records, field boundaries and field names on maps of 1782 and 1839 (3) show they were at the south east corner of the parish adjoining the site of Chadacre Hall. These two areas are shown on Map 1 and according to the Tithe assessment covered a total of 115 acres. They were apparently approached from Hill Farm by a track called 'Woodway'. The area of the Great Wood included a barn or farmhouse formerly known as Hartest Wood, then Hartest Farm and now Lords Farm. Thus the link with the monastic woodland of the Abbot of Ely, as Lord of the Manor is preserved in the present-day name.

In 1729 this small farm carved out of the edge of the wood was leased by Thomas Turner, Lord of the Manor, to William Gallent, clothier. It was then described as 'All that Barn and stable adjoining, with the lands, pasture ground . . . called Hartest Wood'. The lease prohibited the tenant from felling large trees which remained the Lord's property, but he was able to take the 'loppings and toppings of the Pollard trees . . .' He also agreed not to change the balance between pasture and arable land on the farm. Gallent proposed to enlarge a meadow of 1½ acres to 6 acres and to ditch the new boundary '. . . so as not to damage any Trees' (4).

Between the lease in 1729 and the purchase of Hartest Manor by Rev. John Weller Poley in 1782, most of the Great Wood was cleared and divided into enclosures by fairly straight hedges.

One of the farms in the area, possibly the moated site of Rivetts Hall immediately adjacent to Little Wood, was formerly known as 'Stubbards' which implies that former woodland had been cleared.

The village proper is clustered around the central green. This was originally larger as is shown on Map 2. It appears that the eastern edge was formerly on the other side of the river, and that the tightly packed houses along the present eastern edge are later encroachments. Two factors support that conclusion: firstly the earlier community needed more obvious access to the main water supply; secondly the gardens of many of the houses extend beyond the river. A timber-framed Wealden house, between 'Hunters' and

'Green Farm', dates from c.1470, which suggests the encroachment is an early change to the plan of the village.

On the south side of the Green, at the lower end, near the fording point of the river, stands the church, which was already there by 1086; the Hall or Manor House, now the Crown Inn, higher up the slope; and the Rectory to the south of the church. The southern edge has been altered by the encroachment of 'Church Cottage' and the group including 'Curate's House'.

On the western side the Green originally tapered into Somerton Road, as it still does on the north side, into Workhouse Hill. South of Place Farm the modern map still shows a large triangular area, which was once part of the Green. The houses on this triangle date from the 17th to 19th centuries. Evidence from the manorial records indicate that the Lord's pound was situated at this end of the Green.

In common with many parishes in High Suffolk, such as Brockley, Whepstead and Cockfield, Hartest included several groups of houses called 'End' or 'Green' as well as outlying farms. The 1841 census provides the earliest complete list of locations:– South End (formerly Rotten Row), West End and Mile End (Somerton Road); North End (Bury Road); East Hill (Hartest Hill and beyond). The Greens were, Pence or Penns Green, an open area to the east of Hartest Bridge, taking its name from a house called 'Penns'; Cross Green at the top of Workhouse Hill; and Freeds Green, to the east of Freeds or Rogers Lane between Charity Farm and the Wick. In 1327 one Hugo Frede was taxed 2s., and this is the earliest recorded use of the name in Hartest. The area of the Green did not remain stable; in 1712 for example Henry Sparke was presented before the manorial court for 'encroaching upon the waste of this manor by taken in part of the green called freeds green . . .' (5). By 1839 it survived only as Freeds Field on the Tithe Map.

Twenty-four farms were recorded in the 1841 Census. The names of three of them can be traced back at least to 1327, when Henry Waryn, Robert the Long and Robert of Monte (Mount or Hill) all appear among the list of tax payers (6).

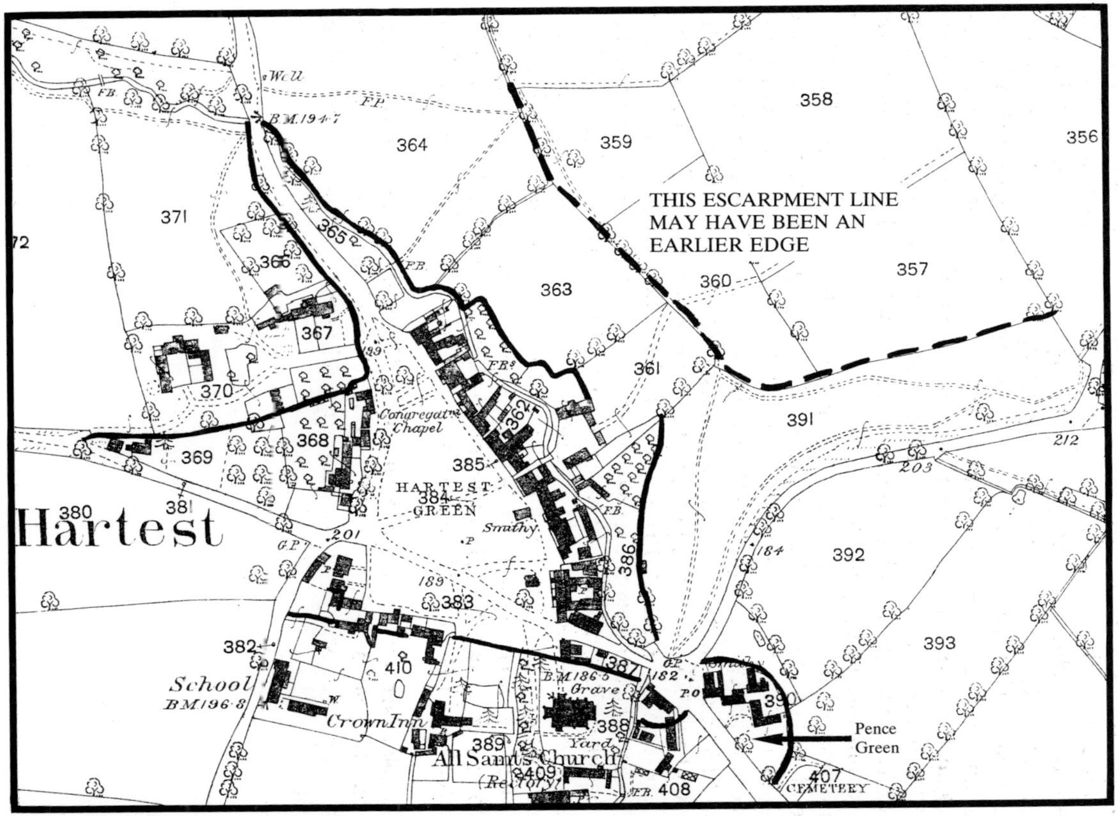

Map 2. Showing the suggested earlier boundaries of the Green. Base map reproduced from 1884 Ordnance Survey 25″ to 1m sheet Suffolk (West) LX111.2.

Ploughing in October: from 'A Book of Divers Devices' by Thomas Fella of Dunwich (1585–1622).

Agriculture

A 17th century writer described the heavy clay-loam area of High Suffolk as being '. . . enclosed for pasture grounds, employed most to grazing and dairy . . .' (1). This general comment is refined by Robert Ryece of Preston: '. . . those parts including to the east having sufficient tillage, abound with all meadow and pasture by reason whereof their greatest commodities are raised by feeding and grasing . . . The midle parts of the country are rich in pasture and plenty of meddowes butt their chiefest is corne grounds from all which riseth the gain that filleth their purses . . .' (2). It is in this latter area that Hartest is situated.

Ryece also described the good agricultural practice of giving the ground a summer tilth every third year. '. . . the good husband that ever desireth to make his crop, which though it happeneth to prove cheap, yett being plentifull far exceedeth for profitt the proportion of other years when corne is att a higher price. Having thus done to give more strength and courage to his ground, hee giveth the same another summer tilth, which though for every acre it may stand him above 26s, yett is he thus commonly sure of a good crop of cleane graine . . .' (3).

A Terrier and Survey of Boxted Manor in 1630 shows that a similar rotation was specified in the leases of the manorial land (4). In the Terrier each of the farms are described and extracts from the leases added in another hand.

The New Dayrie House farm, for instance was hired by Samuel Granger for seven years from Michaelmas 1629. The land amounted to 206 acres of which 141 were meadow or pasture and 65 arable. The tenant was allowed '. . . To take but two crops together & then summer tyll, except a third cropp of pease. To leave 20 acres fallow, and to have for every earth (ploughing) 3s. 4d. & abate (reduction) of rent 9s. per acre . . .'.

Braggins farm in Boxted was 165 acres in extent. The lease included a very significant clause. '. . . The Tennant . . . not to take above 2 cropps of corn together, but shall follow & summer tyll according to the custome of the Country; a third cropp of peason to be taken upon any of the said lands after 2 other cropps of any other graine there taken one yeare immediatelie after another . . .'.

The summer tilth would enable the land to rest and recover, and the alternative of a crop of peas would put nitrogen back into the soil. The farmers may not have understood the scientific reasons for growing peas, but they understood its beneficial effects.

This tilth and a second ploughing, known as the 'after tilth', was included in the probate valuations just as land ploughed is valued today when farms are sold. In August 1650, the after tilth of 9½ acres was worth £1 (5); in January 1665 the '. . . tylth of land that is unsown & the last years rent . . .' came to £8, with the after tilth at £1 (6); in August 1678 the '. . . rent & tilth of the plowed land, and the after tilth . . .' came to £4 10s. (7); in November 1705, the tilth of 5 acres of land was valued at £4 10s., the rent £3 10s. and the after tilth at £2 2s. (8).

Crops

The main sources for the details of crops and livestock are Probate Inventories. These are detailed valuations of the goods and chattels of a person who has recently died. For Hartest there are 26 such inventories giving details of crops in 1616, 1650-1710 and 1728. They mention wheat, barley/malt, corn, peas, oats, bullimong and grass/hay.

In percentage terms, wheat was mentioned in 69% of the inventories; barley and malt in 50%, unspecified corn in a further 26% not having wheat or barley; peas in 26%; oats in 11%; bullimong (a mixture of grains) in 15%; and grass or hay in 84%. Fruit and hops were also grown although not mentioned in any detail.

According to the time of year that the inventory was taken the crops were either valued as a harvested crop by the load, parcell, coomb or bushell, or as a growing crop by the acre 'on the ground'.

Just as today, wheat was sown before Christmas. Valuations made between January and April had both grain from the previous year's harvest, and wheat sown in the ground. This wheat was valued at £3 an acre in February 1652. Wheat growing in June 1700 was worth £2 10s. an acre, and just before harvest in August 1703 at £3 acre. Harvested wheat was valued at 9s. 2d. a coomb in April 1703, 15s. a coomb in August 1703, and 17s. 5d. a coomb in March 1728. The area under the crop ranged from 1¼ to 6 acres.

Barley was valued at £2 an acre in June 1700, compared with £2 10s. for wheat; and at 11s. a coomb in March 1728, compared with 17s. 5d. for wheat. The area under the crop ranged from 1¼ to 5 acres, although 9 acres were mentioned in the will of Robert Frost in 1574 (9).

Unspecified corn was valued at £1 an acre in the will of Edmund Copping (10) in 1601. A century later, in 1703, 6 acres belonging to Ann Cranshaw (11) were valued at £1 6s. 8d. an acre.

The only valuations of bullimong were 18s. an acre in July 1667, and at 3s. 6d. a coomb in April 1703.

Grass and the resulting hay, were an important crop providing the grazing and feed for the large number of livestock, especially the horses and cattle which appear to have formed the basis of the farming economy. Six acres of grass were worth 14s. an acre in April 1703. The hay was usually described as a 'parcell' or 'in the barn'. However, John Frost (12), a tanner, in 1663 had 12 Jags (small cart loads), and a Cock or stack of hay belonging to William Stern (13), was valued at £4 2s. 6d. in 1679.

There is evidence that hops were also grown in Hartest. John Frost (12) had hop poles in his yard in 1663. Benjamin Lilly (14) a wheelwright, had a sack of hops in his attic in 1667. He lived on the east side of the green near 'Hunters' where there was a piece of land called 'Little Hop Ground'.

Sowing winter wheat: from ‘A Book of Divers Devices’ by Thomas Fella of Dunwich (1585–1622).

The only evidence of clover comes from the inventory of Thomas Cronshay (15) in 1700, when a clover sieve is mentioned.

Our only information of the relative acreages of various crops on a single farm comes from the same inventory when in 1700 Cronshay had 6 acres of wheat, 5 acres of barley, 4 acres of bullimong, 6 acres of grass and ¾ acre of peas. An interesting comparison is found in the inventory of William Shelly (16) in 1703 when a coomb of harvested wheat and a rood, or quarter of an acre, of wheat growing in the field, were both valued at 15s. This would therefore give a yield of about four coomb an acre in 1703.

Livestock

Livestock is mentioned in 24 Probate Inventories covering the period 1616-1728. In percentage terms, cattle were mentioned in 91% of the inventories; horses in 75%, pigs in 66%; sheep in 20% and poultry in 16%.

Cattle were described as cows, milch neat, bulls, bullocks and calves. Cows were valued at £3 5s. each in 1675 and 1703; at £2 15s. in 1705 and £3 16s. in 1728. Calves were worth 15s. in 1650 and a weaned calf at 9s. in 1703. The cows were obviously for dairying and the bullocks for fattening.

Horses included mares, colts and a nagg or small riding horse. They were worth between £1 2s. 6d. and £3 each in 1704-5; a blind mare £1 in 1728. The working horses were used for pulling agricultural equipment and various types of wheeled vehicles. There are many references to horse harness, collars and traces made of leather or hemp. Other horses were obviously used for riding or as pack animals and there are numerous references to different types of saddles.

Pigs were described as pigs, swine, shoats or half-grown pigs, sows and hogs or castrated pigs kept for fattening. Most of these animals were kept in small numbers for household consumption and also appeared as bacon in the inventories. Others may have been kept for fattening and selling on the wider market. Perhaps, as suggested by Joan Thirsk (17) for providing bacon for London and the Navy. Randal Lock (18) in 1710 had at least 2 sows and 11 pigs, and is the largest producer known in Hartest.

Sheep were kept in small numbers. In 1616 Thomas Cronshay (19), the Rector, had 25 valued at 5s. each; in 1663 John Frost (20), tanner, had 17 sheep and lambs valued at £3; in 1700 Edward Johnson (21), gentleman, had 2 sheep and 2 lambs; in 1703 Ann Cranshaw (22), widow, had 14 sheep and 10 lambs valued at £4 10s.

Poultry was rarely noted by the appraisers making the inventory. They were never totalled, probably because, like the 'lumber' in the house, they were insignificant, and were usually described as 'poultry in the yard'.

It would seem likely that beekeeping was common in the 17th century. But only three references to them can be found. The will of Thomas Goshawk (23), Yeoman, in 1629, mentions '. . . three hives of Bees with the stooles whereon they stand . . .'; Richard Cronshay (24), gentleman, in 1685 had '. . . bees & fowlls in the yard . . .'; and an earlier will of James Hibble (25) in 1569 mentions '. . . two hyves with bees . . .'.

Sowing barley in March: from 'A Book of Diverse Devices' by Thomas Fella of Dunwich (1585–1622).

The high percentage of cattle, grass and hay shows that dairying was the major element in the economy of Hartest. The number of cows in individual ownership ranged from two, which may have been just for domestic use, up to a herd of 15 owned by Randal Lock (26) in 1710. Among his possessions Randal also had cheese amounting to 9½ weigh (or wey). A weigh varied between 312 and 336 lb. This cheese therefore was either 2,964 or 3,192 lb, being valued at about 1½d. a lb. On average each cow produced milk sufficient for between 197 and 212 lb. of cheese.

Cheese and butter making was carried out extensively and most houses had some of the necessary utensils such as trays, pans, pails, tubs, bowls, churns and cream pots. Perhaps the most common were milk killers or shallow trays for cooling and skimming the milk. Some of them were described as 'standing', one was made of stone, another was 'a lead to set milk'.

To process the cheese they used cheese presses (weighed down with stones or operated by a screw), cheese motts or fats (vats or moulds in which cheese was shaped), cheese breads (covers), cheese tongs, and scales and weights for weighing the cheeses.

To process butter were churns, one described as a 'hand churn' and two as 'barrell chirns', butter killers, firkins (barrels holding 56 lb. butter) and butter scales and weights.

As we saw earlier, cheese was often stored in local farmhouses, awaiting sale or collection and included in the inventories. In 1664 15 cheeses were valued at 1s. each; Robert Cronshay (27) had 139 in his cheese chamber in 1665; and William Shelly (28) had 78 small cheeses at 1s. each in 1703.

Apart from the firkin mentioned previously, butter was only mentioned in general terms.

Implements

In the barns, stables and outhouses the larger agricultural implements were to be found. These included ploughs, with plough irons and coulters, harrows and 'rowles' (rollers) with all the various harnesses and traces. Carts were the most frequently mentioned vehicle. Some were obviously East Anglian hermaphrodite waggons, as there are references to 'a cart and a pair of wheels'. An extension including an axle and wheels was added to the front of a specially designed cart, and it became a waggon. This type of cart-waggon seems to have been common in Hartest, as, although several tumbrells are mentioned, only one waggon is recorded. Ladders were frequently listed and, apart from the usual meaning, were extensions fitted to the front and back of carts to enable a larger load to be carried. These would be especially necessary with the hermaphrodite cart.

Hand tools for reaping included the scythe, mainly used for the hay harvest; the sickle with its serrated blade, which was the principal cutting tool before the 19th century; and the reaping hook. Other harvest tools were the wooden swath rake, for gathering up the cut hay or corn, and the pitchfork.

Corn was threshed with a flail, and then winnowed with a 'casting shovel' or

Killing swine in December: from 'A Book of Diverse Devices' by Thomas Fella of Dunwich (1585–1622).

a 'fan' (a flat fan-shaped basket with handles) and a 'screen' (a large rectangular sieve). A final process was sieving with a 'chaff sieve'. Other crops were separated using a riddle or a clover sieve.

Various containers for storage and measuring were kept in the barns and houses. These included sacks, maunds (baskets), bushels, pecks and half pecks.

Hand tools for work on the land included spades, 'shod shovels' (wooden shovels with an iron cutting edge), shovels, forks, mattocks, wooden and iron rakes, and a bush scythe.

Several tools for working with wood were listed, such as saws, hatchets, axes, 'hagsaws', handsaws, iron wedges and beetles (iron bound wooden mallets).

Horsemills and the mill house in which they stood, were mentioned in wills and inventories from 1559-1700. Three generations of the Cronshay family in 1616, 1664 and 1700 had 'a horse mill in the millhouse'. Thomas Alban had a horsemill and a windmill near Freeds Green in 1583. This is the earliest reference to a windmill in Hartest, and it was either located near Mill End Farm along Somerton road, or near the site of the former mill at Mill Farm.

Pruning trees in March: from 'A Book of Diverse Devices' by Thomas Fella of Dunwich (1585–1622).

Cloth Trade

Occupational evidence from wills and inventories for the 17th century shows that Hartest had clothiers, staplers, yeomen, weavers, websters and woolcombers all connected with the cloth trade. The raw wool was mainly imported from other parts of England, treated, combed and spun into yarn in Hartest and the surrounding villages and then sent to London and Norwich '. . . where it is ever readily sold to those who make thereof all sorts of fringes, stuffs and many other things which are at this day used and worn.' (1).

The clothiers, staplers and yeomen of Hartest employed local people in various processes. In addition they gave work to weavers in Stanstead, sheremen in Glemsford and supplied finished yarn to Cavendish and Norwich.

John Frost senior, who died in 1609, was engaged in the broadcloth trade (2). His executor was to pay his wife £10 '. . . out of twoe broad clothes now at the weavers, whereof one Cloth is in the Custodye of John Cawston of Stanstead, weaver and the other clothe is now in the custody of one Permesy of Hartest aforesaid weaver . . .'. He also leaves his son '. . . one Russett broad cloth, and one dozen and a half of Twill now lyenge at the house of Thomas Hardy, sherman, in Glemsford . . .'. Among the residue of his estate are both wool and yarn.

Thomas Underwood junior in 1661 had no stated occupation, but the items listed in his inventory show him to have been a clothier (3). He had 448 lb. of 'flece wooll' in its raw state and various types and remnants of combed wool. These included 200 lb. of 'saye cast wooll'; 120 lb. of 'handwarpe wooll'; 38 lb. of 'midle wooll'; 160 lb. of 'say nills' (niles, short wool left in the comb after the long fibres have been removed); 20 lb. of 'fine nills'; 20 lb. of 'short wooll'; 180 lb. of 'topps of comed woole' (combed wool ready for spinning) and 80 lb. of 'forcins'. The finished yarn amounted to 29 gross or a staggering 4,176 lb. Other items included six bushels of charcoal, used for heating wool combs, and a gallon of oil, for rubbing into the wool during combing. He also had two leeps (large deep baskets for wool), two hardills (wooden implement in which teasles are mounted) two pack-cloths capable of holding 240 lb. of wool each, a malling cord and a saddle.

The wool, yarn and equipment amounted to £83 5s.8d. or 56.4% of his total wealth while the household goods came to £5 8s.2d. or 3.1%. It is possible that the appraisers ignored other household goods. The debts owed to him totalled £59 0s. 3d. or 40.2% of the total value: £4 3s. 3d. of that amount was owed 'at norwich', giving us firm evidence that he was sending yarn there; £11 was owed by two men from Cavendish.

William Underwood, cousin of Thomas, was described as a clothier in his inventory of 1678 (4). He had '. . . woll and Yarne and tops and pac-Clothes . . .' worth £190, which represents 45% of the total value of his

PROBATE INVENTORY OF THOMAS UNDERWOOD

March the 1 1660

A trew and perfitt Inventory of all the goods and Chattells
that Thomas Underwod the yongr of Hartest
in the County of Suffollk dyed seased of

	£	s	d
Imprimus sixteen tood of flece wooll at 25s. per tood	20	0	0
Itm tenn scor of saye cast wooll at 11d. per pound	10	1	8
Item six scor of handwarpe wooll at 14d.	7	0	0
Item thurty eight pounds of midll woole at 8d. the pound	1	5	4
Item eaight scor pounds of say nills at 4d. the pound	2	13	4
Item Nine scor topps of Comed woolle at 18d. the pound	13	10	0
Item twenty nine groc of yarne at 16s. the groce	23	4	0
Item one scor of fine nills at 6d. the pound	0	10	0
Item one scor of short wooll at 7d. the pound	0	11	8
Item 6 bushill of Charcolle at 12d. the bushill	0	6	0
Item one gallon of oyle at 3s.8d. the galon	0	3	8
Item two leeps and 2 hardills	0	5	0
Item 2 pack Cloths and a malling Cord	0	5	0
Item fowr scor pounds of forcins a 1½d. a pound	0	10	0
Item on mare sadle and wonty	3	0	0
Item debts owing him at norwich	43	3	3
Item owing him by lenard Jackson	4	17	0
Item owing him by Bridg and Serlls of Cavendish	11	0	0
Item he left in monys	1	12	2
Item a table	0	16	0
Item his wering Cloths	3	0	0
the sum is	147	14	1

John Jackson
Thomas Payne

SRO(B):IC500/3/5/189

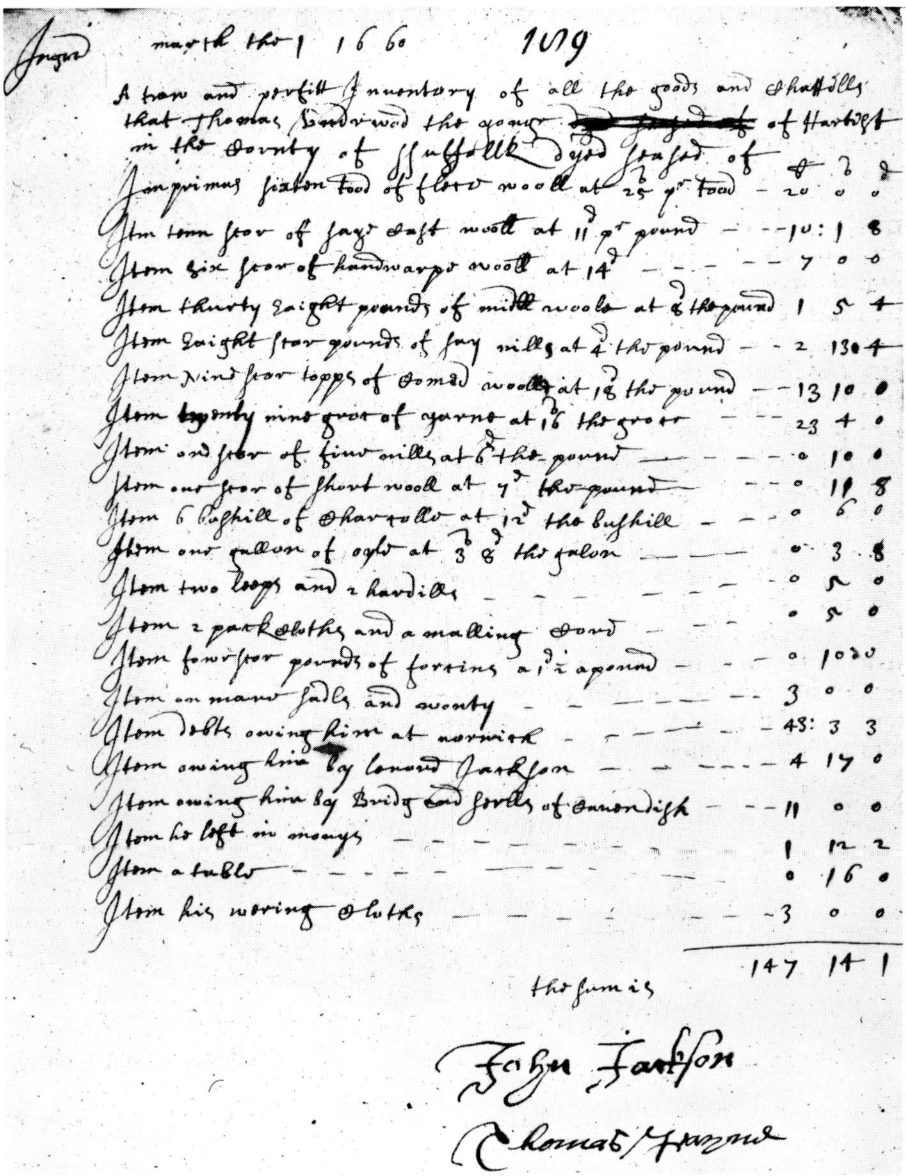
Ingred march the 1 1660 1019

A true and perfitt Inventory of all the goods and Chattells that Thomas Underwood the younger [illegible] of Harleigh in the County of Suffolk dyed seased of

	£	s	d
Inprimus sixteen tood of fleece wooll at 25s pr tood	20	0	0
Item tenn score of fayr east wooll at 11d pr pound	10	1	8
Item six score of handwarpe wooll at 14d	7	0	0
Item thurty eaight pounds of mill woole at 8d the pound	1	5	4
Item eaight score pounds of fay nills at 4d the pound	2	13	4
Item nine score topps of combed wooll at 18d the pound	13	10	0
Item [twenty] nine groce of yarne at 16s the groce	23	4	0
Item one score of fine nills at 6d the pound	0	10	0
Item one score of short wooll at 7d the pound	0	11	8
Item 6 bushill of charcole at 12d the bushill	0	6	0
Item one gallon of oyle at 3s 8d the galon	0	3	8
Item two loops and 2 hardills	0	5	0
Item 2 packclothes and a malling cord	0	5	0
Item fowrscor pounds of fortins a 1d ½ a pound	0	10	0
Item on mare sadle and awonty	3	0	0
Item debts owing him at norwich	48	3	3
Item owing him by Leonard Jackson	4	17	0
Item owing him by Bridg and Jewels of Cavendish	11	0	0
Item he left in moneys	1	12	2
Item a table	0	16	0
Item his wearing clothes	3	0	0
the sum is	147	14	1

John Jackson

Thomas Hayward

goods. His widow Elizabeth (5), who died later the same year had '. . . yarne and tops at spinninge' valued at £20.

James Jackson (6), a stapler, in 1678 had 7 pack cloths and an iron winch in the chamber over the entrance of his house. Could this winch have been used to haul wool up to a storage room on the first floor? In the buttery were five spinning wheels and a reel (for winding the spun wool), and in the buttery chamber a pair of scales and 14 lb. of lead weights. He also had wool valued at £60, which represents 48% of his moveable wealth.

William Bray, a weaver, in 1639, owned houses in Sudbury and bequeathed to each of five nephews and nieces '. . . soe much of my woollen cloths as shall be reasonably worth forty shillings' (7). Richard Parnasy, a weaver who was mentioned in the earlier will of John Frost, died in 1644. However, neither his will, nor those of John Hayward, weaver, in 1652, and Robert Enos, say weaver in 1684, mentioned any wool or cloth.

Wool combers are mentioned in Hartest wills 1671-1690, but none bequeathed any goods associated with their trade. Later, in 1707, John Metcalf, a wool comber, had '. . . yarne & toopes, . . . skales and waites . . . wool . . . nepings and clothes . . . niles, Ille (oil) and Coole (coal) . . . two pound of hose yarn . . .' (8), all valued at £16 10s. 7d. or 39% of his total wealth.

James Jackson in 1700, and John Bonger in 1701, were both described as yeomen, yet they were both heavily engaged in the cloth trade. James Jackson had '. . . wooll & yarn in the house' (worth £104) . . . oyl in the house . . . Topps in the spinners hands . . . chalf cole . . . scales and weights' (9), all of which were valued at £142 17s. 6d. or 49% of his wealth. This compares with his hay, corn, animals and husbandry necessaries amounting to only £25 12s. 6d. or 8%.

John Bonger had wool, yarn, oil, chaff cole, niles, scales and weights in his house, and tops away at the spinners (10), all worth £29 14s. 6d. or 69% of his total valuation.

William Shelly (11), in 1703, seems to have been a yeoman. Yet he also had a combing shop containing two pairs of combs, a wool skeep (basket) and coals, while in the Hall were three wheels and a reel. Although the value of these goods only represented 0.5% of his total wealth, their presence shows that combing was an additional source of income.

Population

17th century tax lists and surveys of church attendance provide the historian with statistics from which to calculate very approximate estimates of the population. This is no easy task and the study of demography is hedged around with pit-falls.

The baptismal register (1) has been analysed from 1600-1700 in order to establish the trends in population from decade to decade. The method used for this has been to total the baptisms for a decade, find the average and multiply by 30. The same method has also been used for 1596-1704, over nine year periods in order to suggest a figure for each year of the century. It must be stated at the outset that these figures can only give basic trends, and cannot be relied upon for any single year.

The trends revealed by the decennial analysis show a sharp rise in population in the period 1610-19 to an average of 492, compared with 399 in the previous decade 1600-9; a slight increase to 522 in the 1620s, and a further rise to 588 in the 1630s. The population reached its peak for the 17th century in the 1640s with a further increase to an average of 612.

In the 1650s there was a dramatic fall to 492, which does not seem to be accounted for either by under-registration or high mortality. The population then rose again for the next three decades, averaging 516 in 1660s, 558 in the 1670s and 594 in the 1680s. In the final decade of the century the population fell to much the same level as in the 1670s an average of 546.

Graph to show population trends 1600–1700.

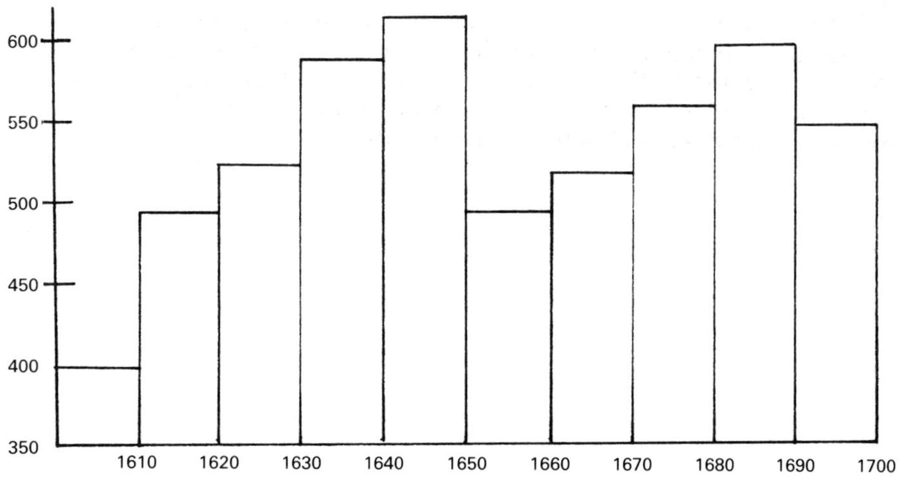

The Ecclesiactical Census of 1603 can also be used for population history (2). The clergy had to send the Bishop details of the number of communicants, nonconformists and Roman Catholics over sixteen years old in their parish.

Unfortunately Hartest and Boxted are given as a single total of 320 communicants. A similar survey in 1676 gives the total separately for each parish. The proportion of communicants in Hartest and Boxted was then about six-to-one. Assuming, and it may be wrong to so assume, that the population in both parishes had increased at the same rate, then we can speculate that in 1603 Hartest had about 270 communicants and Boxted about 45. Recent research by Wrigley and Schofield (3) suggests that 49.7% should be added to the base figure for those adults omitted from the survey and those under sixteen years old. This calculation gives a total figure of about 404 for Hartest, which corresponds closely with the average for that decade of 399 and an estimate for 1603 of 383.

In 1608 because of their poverty the copyholders of Hartest Manor petitioner the Crown not to increase the manorial fines and rents (4). The petition shows that some forty copyholders had land of two acres or less and a further thirty-five had neither land nor homes of their own. Thus at least seventy five families could be regarded as being poor.

The estimate from the register for 1608 is 463. To turn this figure into families we need to divide by 4.3 as the size of the average family. This gives a total of 107 families of which 75, or 70% comprised the poor members of the community.

In 1651 another petition, this time for the repair of the church tower, enables a further estimate of the population to be made (5). The petitioners stated that of the 144 families in Hartest, 100 were 'receivers' of poor relief, and the other 44 'mean inhabitants' were only of average wealth. Thus in 1651 69% of the families in Hartest were regarded as the poor, a percentage which is remarkably close to that of 1608. It would seem the community had a large proportion of poor families for at least the first half of the 17th century.

The Hearth Tax of 1674 records 72 individual households or families for Hartest (6). In common with 60% of the other parishes in Babergh Hundred, the poor or those 'certified for' were not included in the 'list'. Therefore any calculation of population based on the Hearth Tax would be spurious.

The Compton Census of 1676 again gives details of the number of communicants, nonconformists and Roman Catholics over sixteen years of age. The original return made by the Rector to the Bishop has survived and gives a total of 392 communicants in Hartest (7). The recommended methods of estimating the population are to either add 31% or 40% to the base figure. This gives us either 513 or 548 as the approximate population, which is again very close to both 558 as the average for the 1670's, and 543 as the estimate for 1676.

Many of the statistics and resulting calculations may be serious under-estimates of the population. However, the general trends, based on the baptismal register, do appear to be supported by the other sources.

The Church before the Reformation

There had been a church in Hartest at least since c.1086, when the Domesday jurors declared there to be a church with 80 acres of land.

The present building consists of a 14th century chancel, south aisle and chapel; 15th century north aisle and chapel, and a 16th century north porch. The tower is basically 14th century, with upper stages rebuilt in the 1650s.

Isaac Johnson's drawing of the church in 1818, shows a window in the south wall of the chancel, which was blocked up some time between the visit of David Davy in 1831 and the restoration of 1879. This is the window to which John Marleton in 1529, butcher, bequeathed £1 '. . . to the makynge of the new windowe at the southe end of the heye alter . . .' (1). The outline of the window can still be clearly seen from outside the church. Remarkably, the mullions and tracery are still preserved, sealed in the thickness of the wall. They can be seen by looking into and above the internal piscina, which must have been in the original window sill.

Hartest Church, drawn by Isaac Johnson, 1818.

The south chapel was described in the 15th and 16th centuries as the 'chapel of the Blessed Mary', and 'the chapel situated in the church yard of Hartest'. This indicates that it was built as an addition to the existing chancel and aisle, and on ground which had formerly been part of the churchyard. Further evidence for this interpretation comes from both the distinctive angle buttresses and the alignment of the south wall, which is built two feet six inches further south than that of the aisle. Inside the chapel stood an image, or statue, of the Virgin Mary. Hartest people made bequests to paint the image, to maintain lights burning before it and to repair the chapel.

Although the south side is furthest away from the main centre of the community, the aisle on this side is older than on the north. The roof appears to have been carved and decorated without an overall scheme, suggesting that it may have been paid for a bay at a time as funds and donations permitted. Two bays have a carved pomegranate, which usually represents Catherine of Aragon, Queen of England 1509-1533. In the north-east angle of the porch is a filled-in holy water stoup, which indicates that this was the main entrance to the church.

The north aisle has a set of later windows with horizontal transoms. In 1528 a bequest of 6s. 8d. was left '. . . towards the battlement of the north part of Hartest church,' (2) which might refer to the aisle. One of the western bays of the roof has a carved mullet or star in the spandrel, which could either indicate the de Vere family of Lavenham, or the Drurys of Rougham and Hawstead. John de Vere, thirteenth Earl of Oxford, left money in 1513 to the church of every parish in which he owned land, which may have included Hartest. Roger Drury of Hawstead in 1494, bequeathed money to local churches including Hartest where he certainly had land.

The north porch has a small shield either side of the entrance, one with the letters 'JPſ' and the other 'Anna'. These are probably John Phillipson senior, and Ann his wife. John, a yeoman, in 1546 requested to be buried '. . . within the porch on the Northsyde of Hartest church.' (3) These two pieces of evidence suggest that he paid for its building during his lifetime.

The earliest reference to the Rood Loft at Hartest is 1471, when William Hall gave 13s. 4d. to the making '. . . of the Rode Loft in Harthurst church.' (4) This structure was replaced in the 1520s when a series of large bequests were made towards the making and painting of a new loft. In 1519 John Gardiner gave '. . . to the makynge off a new Rodeloft in the said churche of herthurst £3 6s. 8d. to be paid whan the sayd Rodeloft soshalbe begune & the other £3 6s. 8d. when ytt ys endyng . . .' (5). John Mancer who was curate of Shimpling, in 1521 left 6s. 8d. to the '. . . Rood painting . . .' (6). Thomas Gardiner a further £6 13s. 4d. in 1524 (7), and the final recorded bequest was in 1528 when £6 13s. 4d. was to be used '. . . towards the making of the roodloft . . .' (8). Part of the screen which supported the loft has survived, and now forms part of the front bench in the nave.

A bequest was made to the holywater clerk in 1431. He was a member of a minor holy order, presumably responsible for keeping the stoup filled and carrying a holy water pail in procession (9). In 1494 and 1496 there were gifts of money for painting a canopy over the high altar (10), and for making a tabernacle (a carved frame and canopy, to contain and show off an image) over the high altar (11). The tabernacle containing the image of St Thomas was repainted in 1492 (12), and a bequest made for repairing the chapel of St. Nicholas in 1535 (13).

The series of bequests on which this section has been based, gives only a partial picture of the fabric and contents before the reformation. The section on 'Beyond the Grave' contains details of pre-reformation belief, and the sections on the 'Fall of the Tower' and the 'Restoration of 1879' complete the history of the church.

The Civil War

Frederick Gibb: Rector of Hartest and Boxted

In the spring of 1642 Parliament and the King were drawing further and further apart, as each side tried to gain support for the seemingly inevitable conflict.

One of the major confrontations arose over the legality and right to muster, or call up, the militia and to raise money for its support. The ancient method was for the King to send a document called the 'Commission of Array' to the Lord Lieutenant of each county. But in February 1642, Parliament nominated its own Lord Lieutenants and in March issued an Ordinance, or decree, ordering them to call up and raise money for the militia.

However, the Ordinance was not enforced in the hope that the King would eventually agree to the supremacy of Parliament. In May the King issued a declaration against the Militia Ordinance, stating that '. . . there was no legal power in either, or Houses, (of Parliament) upon any pretence whatsoever, without his Majesty's consent . . .' (1). Subsequent declarations and countermands were issued by both sides throughout June and July 1642.

In the midst of this confusion, Frederick Gibb, who had been Rector since 1627, found himself being drawn into confrontation with Parliament. The following account of the events is drawn from the House of Lords Archives, the Journal of the House of Commons and a Royalist newsbook called 'Mercurius Rusticus'.

On Sunday morning the 10 July 1642, before he was to preach the sermon, Frederick Gibb told the congregation that he was going to read out the King's declaration against one of the Militia Ordinances, whereupon he was interrupted by Edward Colman gentleman, who said that Gibb '. . . might be ashamed to abuse the people by reading his Majestys declarations to them, and therefore he would fetch him some Parliamentary declarations which were a great deal better to be published unto them.'

Gibb again attempted to read the declaration, and was again prevented by Colman saying, 'Well then Sir, you mean to be an obedient servant of his Majesty' to which Gibb replied 'Yes, Sir, I am, and hope to continue a faithfull servant unto him as long as I live'. He then proceeded to read the King's declaration, which was according to the Royalist newsbook, was well received by the congregation '. . . standing very attentive to heare it'. Colman the spoke up again saying, 'Well Sir, the King neither is nor shall be the Judge of the law, whatever such parting fellows as you would have him' (2).

Edward Colman, and John Grigg another parishioner, went to London and reported the events to the House of Commons on 21 July 1642 (3). The Serjeant at Arms was ordered to arrest Gibb and bring him to the House for further examination. Colman and Grigg had obviously arrived in London before 18 July, as a newsheet of that date reported the details of the incident

By these two places of the holy Scriptures, it is most evident that Kings, Queenes, and other Princes (for he speaketh of authority, and power, be it in men or women) are ordayned of GOD, are to be obeyed, and honoured of their subiects: that such subiects, as are disobedient or rebellious against their Princes, disobey GOD, and procure their owne damnation: that the government of Princes is a great blessing of God, given for the Common-wealth, specially of the good, and godly: For the comfort, and cherishing of whom, God giveth, and setteth up Princes: and on the contrary part, to the feare, and for the punishment of the evill, and wicked. Finally, that if servants ought to obey their masters, not onely being gentle, but such as be froward: as well, and much more ought subiects to be obedient, not onely to their good, and courteous, but also to their sharpe, and rigorous Princes. It becommeth therefore neyther of chance, and fortune (as they terme it) nor of the ambition of mortall men, and women climing up of their owne accord to dominion, that there be Kings, Queenes, Princes, and other Governours over men being their subiects: but all Kings, Queenes, and other Governours are specially appoynted by the ordinance of GOD. And as GOD himselfe, being of an infinite Maiesty, power, and wisedome, ruleth, and governeth all things in Heaven, and Earth, as the universall Monarch, and onely King, and Emperour over all, as being onely able to take, and beare the charge of all: so hath he constituted, ordayned, and set earthly Princes over particular Kingdomes, and Dominions in earth, both for the avoyding of all confusion, which else would be in the world, if it should be without governours, and for the great quiet, and benefit of earthly men their subiects, and also that the Princes themselues, in authority, power, wisedome, providence, and righteousnesse in government of people, and Countreys committed to their charge, should ressemble his heavenly governance, as the Maiesty of heavenly things may by the basenesse of earthly things be shadowed, and resembled, And for that similitude, that is betweene the heavenly Monarchy, and earthly kingdomes well governed, our Saviour Christ in sundry parables sayth, that the kingdome of Heaven is resembled unto a man, a King:

Extract from 'An Homily Against Disobedience and Wilfull Rebellion. 1635 edition.

and added that Gibb had '. . . asserted that he would spend his blood for the declaration' (4).

While all this was happening, Gibb seems to have made a tactical withdrawal from the parish, and was away when '. . . a Messenger was at his house to enquire for him . . .'. He later went to London, surrendered himself to the Serjeant at Arms, and on 1 October submitted a petition to the House of Commons. In it he declared he had '. . . noe intent to give cause of offence to any . . .' and that '. . . he never heard of any order or direction from parliament to the Contrary before his publishinge thereof' (5).

On 5 October the House of Commons ordered him to pay £30 as surety of his future good behaviour. His case was then passed to the Committee for Information for further investigation (6).

Gibb seems to have been removed or ejected from the living of Hartest and Boxted under the Ordinance of January 1644 for the removal or sequestration of 'scandalous clergy'. He had certainly gone by December 1644 when a fifth of his estate was granted for the support of his two children (7).

Richard Duckworth became Rector in February 1650, following the death of Frederick Gibb. Duckworth was at Hartest in October 1648 when his daughter Martha was buried. Another daughter Susan, was married to Samuel Gibson 'minister' in April 1649.

The register book ceases to be in Gibbs' handwriting on 27 May 1642, with a new hand, possibly that of Duckworth starting on 12 June. It seems probable that Gibb was suspended from office in the autumn of 1642, that Duckworth or other ministers performed the services and subsequently he copied up the details at a later date.

At the restoration of Charles II in 1660 Duckworth was confirmed as Rector, but not before he had to answer charges that he had '. . . used rude expressions against the late King' (8). He remained as Rector of Hartest and Boxted until his death in March 1673.

Ambrose Dister: Churchwarden of Hartest

At the Court of the Archdeaconry of Sudbury, held at Bury St Edmunds on 13 December 1664, charges were heard against Ambrose Dister a former churchwarden of Hartest, who lived until 1645 at Place Farm (9). He was accused, and confessed, that during the Civil War he '. . . did pull downe or cause to bee pulled downe the Font of the said Church', but denied he 'converted any stone, or any other part of the lead, or other Materialls belonging to the said Font, to his use' (10).

His defence was that he did it '. . . out of feare, and by the colour of an Order of some of the Earle of Manchesters souldiers lying then in and about Hartest.'

This statement helps us to date the event, as the Earl of Manchester was General of the Eastern Counties 1642-45. William Dowsing was appointed Parliamentary Visitor by Manchester in December 1643. His task was to enforce an Ordinance of August 1643, ordering the removal from churches of '. . . images and pictures of Saints and superstitious inscriptions . . .' (11).

Charles I: from 'A Brief Remembrance of English Monarchs by John Taylor (1630).

Dowsing's diary records that he was at Glemsford on 26 February 1644, and at nearby Boxted and Somerton on 15 April, when he ordered 'superstitious' pictures to be removed from the windows of both churches.

In May 1644 Parliament passed a second Ordinance for '. . . further demolishing of Monuments of Idolatory and Superstition . . .' (12). Among the items to be 'utterly defaced' were 'Holy-water Fonts'. In many churches the carvings on the fonts were defaced as at Westhall, or plastered over as at Lackford.

The earlier Ordinance had made the Churchwardens responsible for carrying out the order, on pain of a fine of £2 to be paid to the poor. The threat of this fine, the visit of William Dowsing to the area a few weeks earlier, and the presence of Parliamentary troops, probably all combined to make Ambrose Dister act over zealously and order the font to be destroyed.

We can assume, in common with Puritan practice, that a small basin was used at the baptismal services throughout the period of the Commonwealth. The Act of Uniformity in 1662 reinstated the liturgy of the Anglican Church and fonts were once more required for Baptism. The lack of a font at Hartest no doubt led to local enquiries by the church authorities, and someone laid the blame on Ambrose Dister. But without that accusation this interesting event would have gone unrecorded.

Death

In common with all communities, the inhabitants of Hartest were subject to recurring outbreaks of fever, smallpox and plague. These crisis years, or 'visitations' as they were often described in local parish registers, can be identified by the larger number of deaths recorded in individual months or years. Bad harvests and the resulting scarcity of food until the next harvest, were also factors affecting the death rate.

Parish registers present difficulties as a reliable source, as human error may result in some burials not being recorded. Therefore the totals can only be taken to represent the minimum number for each month or year. However, there are no gaps in registration during the Civil War and Commonwealth periods, when many of the highest totals are recorded.

The first crisis of the 17th century occurred in 1601 between 10 November and 18 December when five adults and a child died, compared with thirteen for the whole year.

Between 6 March and 3 April 1606 three adults and a child died, out of a total of ten for the year. Two of those who died were related. Edward the son of Abraham Rogers on the 12th and Abraham himself on 3 April.

In 1610, from 4 February to 27 March, the burials of seven adults and four children were recorded out of a total of seventeen for the entire year. The Frost family lost four members, and may indicate that the outbreak of fever was centred on this one family. John Frost was buried on 6 February; his father John Frost senior, a weaver, made his will on the same day and was buried three days later on 9 February; Ambrose was buried on 21 February and finally Ann the wife of John on 17 March.

The years 1623 and 1624 had eighteen and twenty burials respectively, compared with a twenty-year average of nine. The cause of the deaths was what Creighton described as 'malignant spotted fever' (1). It seems to have mainly affected individuals rather than families, and where families were affected the deaths are well spaced out. This suggests the fever lingered for some time, rather than raging fiercely within a few families.

The height of the disease was in October 1623 when six people, two from the same family were buried. Two burials were recorded in November, two in December, three in February and three in April 1624. In this period Edmund Walker lost two of his three children, Alice aged seven was buried on Christmas Eve 1623 and Martha aged five on 11 January 1624. They were followed to the grave by their aunt Elizabeth on 9 February and uncle Thomas on 14 February 1624.

The period 1635-7 has higher than average mortality having eighteen, thirteen and fourteen burials. It seems that the deaths were caused by a combination of fever and plague. Fever was a recurring disease throughout the 17th century, and plague was present locally, at Shimpling and Bury St Edmunds for example, from July 1637 onwards.

'The wretched begger poore The noble Kynge and all Behold death stands at dore for you he now do call'
From: 'A Book of Diverse Devices' by Thomas Fella of Dunwich (1585–1622).

The first twelve days of March 1637 were the height of the disease with five unrelated burials. The Mayhew family was the only one to have suffered losses in succession. Between 28 November 1636 and 11 March there were buried, Prudence on 28 November, Edmund baptised on Christmas Eve and buried on Christmas Day; Alice aged three years on 19 January 1637; Elizabeth aged five years on 9 February and their father Edmund on 11 March 1637.

A further example of the speed of the disease is shown by the will of Frances Reymond. She had no time to make a proper legally witnessed will and so just told those at her bedside the bequests she wished to leave. They later swore the truth of her nuncupative will before a church official, that Frances '. . . being in perfect mind and memory (had) diverse tymes before her death . . .' (2) told them what to do. Frances was buried on 13 January 1637 but unfortunately those who heard her last instructions did not record the date of her statements.

The year 1639 saw twenty unrelated burials, three in March, four in April, three in July and two each in August and November. The cause of this series of deaths was a mixture of fever and smallpox (3). There is evidence for the speed of the disease from the wills of those who died that year. William Bray (4) a weaver, had his will drawn up on 1 April 1639, died and was buried by the 15 April. Thomas How (5) a webster made a nuncupative will 18 August 1639 '. . . being sick of the sickness he dyed'. His burial is not recorded in the parish register. Peter Borham (6) declared his nuncupative will on 4 January 1640 '. . . being in perfect mind and memory, about an hour or two before his death'. He was buried the following day on 5 January.

The period 1648-51 has the second highest number of deaths for the 17th century with twenty-five, twenty-five, eleven and twenty-eight registered burials. In 1648 the highest months were May, July and August in which eight adults and nine children died. Only two families lost more than one member. Henry Hibble was buried 16 May, and his father James on 13 June; Elizabeth Betts and her husband Robert were buried on 21 and 31 August.

During 1649 the highest period of mortality was 11 to 30 May when eight of the twenty-five burials for the year are recorded. The wills of Alice Farrow (6) and John Hibble (7) who died that month have survived. Alice, a widow, made her will 12 May and included the following touching clause 'Item, in regard that Joane my daughter, the wife of Robert Addames, hath bene at some trouble in lookeinge to me in my sickness, and for that I may hereafter be more troublesome unto her, I give and bequeath unto the sayd Joane her Executors and Assignes, All the rest of my goods chattells personal estate and household (goods) whatsoever . . .'. Alice was buried in Hartest churchyard on 29 May 1649.

John Hibble, a yeoman, made his will on 27 April when he was '. . . at this time sick in body . . .'. He was living with his widowed mother at her house called 'Messengers' which according to his father's will, he was to inherit at her death on condition he paid £10 to his brother James. However, both James and his son had died in 1648 (see above). John therefore willed the property to be put in trust, after the death of his mother, for Mary and Elizabeth his nieces and the daughters of James. They did not have long to wait for their inheritance, as John was buried on 30 May and his mother Mary on 2 June 1649.

1651 was a year of nationwide fever epidemic, and in Hartest there were twenty-eight unrelated burials between January and November.

In 1653 thirteen of the twenty burials occurred between January and March. The Palsey or Pawsey family lost three members at this time; Rose age 14, was buried 14 December 1652, Mary aged 16, on New Year's Day 1653, their father Robert the following day, and his widow Rose on 26 March 1653.

The years 1658 and 1659 was another national outbreak of fever, and at Hartest there were fifteen and sixteen burials recorded in the two years. The largest numbers were in March, October, November 1658, January and May 1659. Again the pattern was for individuals rather than members of the same family to fall victim to the disease.

From July to October 1666 the 'Great Plague' was taking its toll of the Hartest community. Neighbouring villages also suffered at the same time. In the Cockfield register 1666 is described as '. . . the sicknesse yeare . . .' (9), and at Shimpling between 15 October and 1 November five persons were recorded as dying '. . . of the plague . . .'. (10). At Hartest there were thirty-three burials in 1666, twenty-seven of which were between 16 July and 26 October, affecting fourteen families. The pattern of deaths within families shows that some died in quick succession, and others with two or three weeks in between.

Elizabeth Payne was buried on 7 September, her son John aged two years, preceded her to the grave on 15 July, and her daughter Elizabeth aged four, followed her on 6 October. Ralph Twidd, gentleman, who had been responsible for overseeing the rebuilding of the church tower in 1651, was buried on 23 August. Two of his children had died before him, Ralph, aged 10 years was buried on 29 July, and Charles aged 8 years, on 14 August. Ann and Robert Cutmer, a married couple were buried on 26 July and 1 August respectively.

Edward Parkin had died in 1663 leaving a widow Prudence and three children, all of whom were to die in 1666. Edward, aged 8, was buried on 21 September; Prudence the widow, and Ambrose, aged 14, were both buried on 24 September and Priscilla, aged 13, followed on 28 September.

In October the family of George Underwood suffered heavily. George the father, aged 36 years was buried on 9 October; Susan, aged 17 months, on 13 October; Rose, aged 5 on 15 October; George aged 10 on 17 October; Thomas, aged 3 on 22 October and finally John aged 8 on 26 October.

Further evidence for the severity of the plague at Hartest comes from the records of the Court of Quarter Sessions. At a meeting held at Bury on 16 July 1666, the Justices had agreed to levy a monthly rate of £100 within West Suffolk. This was to be used for the relief of '. . . Hadleigh, Cockfield or any other Towne . . . within the Hundreds of Cosford, Babergh and

LIST OF BURIALS TAKEN FROM HARTEST PARISH REGISTER, 1666

Margaret the daughter of William Boorum	May 17th
John Shealy	July 12th
John the sonn of Edward Payne	July 15th
Susan Cutter	July 16th
Alice Ingell	July 16th
Susan the wife of Richard Halwell	July 17th
Ralph Twidd	July 29th
Ann wiff of Robert Cutmer	July 26th
Robert Cutmer	August 1st
William the sonn of James Parkin	August 7th
Charles the sonn of Ralph Twidd	August 14th
Mr Twidd	August 23rd
Elizabeth wiffe of Edward Paine	September 7th
Edward sonne of the widdow Parkin	September 21st
Prudence Parkin widdow Ambos Parkin her sonne Elizabeth the daughter of Thomas Bayley	all in one day September 24th
Prissilla daughter to Prudence Parkin w(id)	September 28th
Elizabeth the daughter of Edward Payne Hanna the daughter of Tempest Diggerson	Both October 6th
George Underwood	October 9th
Susan the dauter of George Underwood	October 13th
Richard the sonn of John West	October 14th
Ann the wife of William Lilly	October 15th
George the sonn of George Underwoode	October 17th
The wiffe of John West	October 18th
Rose the daughter of George Underwood	October 15th
Thomas the sonn of George Underwood	October 22nd
John the sonn of George Underwood	October 26th
Martha the daughter of George Rysin	November 8th
Racael the daughter of Edmond Walker	November 15th
Sara the daughter of William Underwood	December 4th
Thomas Lilly	December 25th

Risbridge . . . by reason of the plague and pestilence now amongst them' (11).

At the next meeting of the Justices on 8 October the situation had generally worsened and Hartest was included as being in particular need of aid '. . . not only the Townes of Hadleigh and Cockfield are driven to great want for lacke of releife, but allso the Towne of Hartest within this division, being now much visited with the plague, many of the Inhabitants if not timely releived are likely to perish . . .' (12) as indeed many of them did.

After the heavy losses of the last outbreak of the plague the period from 1666-1700 saw several other years of high mortality. In 1669 there was a nationwide epidemic of 'gripping of the guts' or diarrhoea, and at Hartest fifteen adults and five children were buried.

In 1671 measles was the prevailing disease and twenty-two burials were recorded, four of which were the result of childbirth. The remaining eighteen comprised twelve adults and six children. Only the Mayes family had more than one death, William aged 13, being buried on 23 August, and his mother Margaret on 26 August. Robert Godward, a yeoman may have died from the same disease, he made his will on 23 July and was buried on 8 August 1671.

In 1675 there were twenty burials, of which only two were related. Richard Limmer, a yeoman, was buried on 23 January; his widow Margery made her will on 29 January and was buried on 15 February.

Epidemic fever was present in 1678 and 1679 when there were eight and twenty-six burials. William Underwood, a clothier, made his will on 1 August and was buried on 5 August; his widow Elizabeth, who was expecting a baby, made her will on 26 August and was buried with her unborn child on 15 September. This couple died in a year of low mortality, and serve not only to show us the speed of the infection, but also to remind us that disease was an ever present cause of death even in years of low mortality.

In 1679 there were twenty-six burials, comprising eighteen adults and eight children. Only two pairs had the same surname, James Pasy or Pawsey, a widower, was buried 17 April and Christian, a singleman, made his will 11 May and was buried on 21 May. Tempest Dickerson lost two of his children in April, John aged 11 was buried on 22 April and Hannah aged 3 on 28 April.

Smallpox was present in 1681, during which twenty-four burials were recorded, including four as a result of childbirth. John Brand lost two of his children in this year, Mary aged 2 on 30 May and Margaret aged 7 on 20 June.

Smallpox, fever, influenza and diarrhoea continued to be recurrent causes of death in the last two decades of the 17th century. The evidence from Hartest indicates that these diseases affected individuals rather than whole families.

The Grave

Until the Burial Board was formed in 1856 everyone who died in Hartest was buried in the churchyard. No gravestones have survived from the 16th or 17th centuries and it is therefore impossible to locate the burial place of individuals from that period. However, occasionally testators gave specific instructions as to their place of burial. John Marlton, a butcher, in 1529 wished to be buried '. . . nyghe unto the buryall of my wife'. (1). John Copyn, a yeoman, in 1531 asked to be buried in the churchyard '. . . that is to saye at the chancells end by the graves of my father and mother and other our frends' (2).

A rare detail comes from the will of Augustine How, a singleman in 1691, who described the wooden covering to be placed over his grave '. . . a decent and convenient Coffin planck to be framed and sett over my grave standing up at the head and feet . . .' (3). His inventory shows his goods to be worth £276 5s. 0d., his will reveals that he owned land and at least two tenanted houses in Hartest. If people of his wealth were having wooden grave markers, perhaps this helps to explain who so few grave stones proper have survived from the 17th century.

Some members of the community requested to be buried inside the church itself. John Philipson senior, a yeoman, in 1546 asked to be buried '. . . within the porch on the Northside of Hartest Church . . .' (4). It would appear from initials outside the porch that he had paid for its construction during his lifetime. Ann Rokewood singlewoman, in 1572 requested to be buried '. . . in the church of hartest or in the channcell nere to the place wher I was wonte to sytt . . .' (5). William Hall, yeoman, in 1608 wished to be buried '. . . in the South Chapell of Hartest churche . . .' (6).

It was customary for Rectors and Vicars to be buried within the chancel of the church. Thomas Cranshay who died in 1615 was '. . . Parson of the parishe church or rectorie of Hartest cum Boxstedd', was 'to be buried in the Chancell of Hartest.' (7). The only other rector whose will has survived is Richard Duckworth in 1672. He not only made no request as to his place of burial but made no statement of his own belief. Perhaps he thought it was too well known to need repeating again!

And Beyond the Grave

Before the Reformation it was common for people to make bequests to secular or religious clergy, in order to aid the progress of their soul through purgatory. The bequest could be a token payment to make up for forgotten tithes due to the rector of the parish in which they owned land, and as a reminder for the priest to pray for them; or money for a secular priest to sing or say a number of masses for the testator's soul; or money for one of the local houses of Friars at Sudbury, Clare, Babwell (Bury) or Cambridge, to do likewise. Sometimes specific types of masses were requested, such as '. . . 5 massys syngyng in the worshyppe of the 5 wonds of our Lord . . .' (1).

Money was also distributed to those attending the burial service, and the usual commemorations at seven and thirty days. This ensured that a large number of people were, in theory, praying for the health of the soul of the deceased.

All these customs were regarded as 'superstitious' by the Protestant reformers in the reigns of Henry VIII and Edward VI, and were abolished along with many other practices and services.

Edward VI's Injunctions of 1547 ordered that money which would have been formerly given for prayers, was now to be given to the support of the poorer members of the community. 'Poore Mens Boxes' were ordered to be set up in every church. The earliest surviving bequests to the Hartest poor box were in 1563 when Roger Copsey gave 6s. 8d. and Andrew Spark a further 5s. In 1564 Edmund Johnson bequeathed 12d. '. . . to the use of the poore in Harteste to be put in the comon boxe . . .' (2).

The tradition of payments to those attending the funeral, was not so easily extinguished in the mind of the ordinary worshipper. In 1570 Ann Garner, a widow, left 13s. 4d. to be given out on her burial day, and Robert Peele in 1573 gave an unspecified sum '. . . to the poor of hartest and boxted . . .' (3) at his burial. William Gardiner in 1566 in lieu of the earlier custom of a tithe payment, left money, ranging from 6s. 8d. to £2, to the poor people of the seven parishes in which he owned land.

The testament section of a last will and testament included the statement of the testator's belief regarding life beyond the grave. Research by Spufford (4) has shown that this statement depended as much on the views of the priest or scribe writing the document, as on the personal belief of the testator. However, these declarations do enable us to examine the changes in doctrine and belief.

A typical pre-reformation Catholic commendation of the soul had the three elements of God, St Mary and the Saints in Heaven. John Copping, a yeoman, made his testament in 1506 '. . . being in holl mynd and good memory, blissyd be Jhu Seyng the perell of deth draw nye I make and ordeyn and dispose my last wyll and testamet In this wyse ffyrst I comend my Sowle to Almighty god And to our Lady Seynt Mary and to all the holy compeny in hevyn . . .' (5).

After Henry VIII was proclaimed Head of the Church in England in 1534, this was acknowledged in the dating of wills, even though of course the commendation remained Catholic. This development of declaring Henry to be head of both Church and State is shown in the will of Joan Everyde, widow, in 1543 'In the yeare of our Lord god 1543 and in the 34 yeare of the reigne of our Soveraigne Lord Kynge Henry the eight beinge supreme heade imediatly under god both of the Spiritualitie & the Temperaltie . . . I bequeath my soule to god allmightie and to our blessed Ladie Saincte Marie and to all the holy sainctes in heven . . .' (6).

The same formula continued into the reign of Edward VI, as is shown in the testament of James Frost, a husbandman, in 1551, '. . . King Edward the syxte defender of the fayth and of the churche of yngland and Ireland and supreme hed . . . I bequeth my soule to god Allmyghty and to our Lady sent Mary and to all the holly copeney of heven . . .' (7).

Truly Protestant belief with the key elements of election, justification, the saving passion and blood of Jesus, was established in the reign of Edward and Elizabeth. The testament of John Heble in 1559 refers to the elect. 'I bequeth my soull into the hands of almightie god my maker savior and redemer trusting throwe the merits of his glorious passion and mightie resurrection to be partaker of his heavenlie fruition amongs his holie and elect servannts . . .' (8)

The testament of William Mayhew in 1575 refers to justification '. . . I doe willinglye Commende my soule into the mercifull hands of god my heavenlye father Trusteinge assuredlye thorowghe the meryts of Jesus Christ to be saved and therefore I doe committ my bodye to be buried in the parish churchyearde of Hartest, aforesayd hopinge to have a ioyfull resurrectione, throughe Jesus Christ who dyed for my synnes and Rose agayne for my Iustificacione' (9).

The testament of Robert Frost, a smyth, in 1574 refers to the passion and blood of Jesus. 'I doo wyllingly commyt my soule into the hands of god my creatour & redemour trustinge assuredly thorough his marcies and the preciouse merytts and bloud sheding of Jesus chryst to be saved and therefore in suer and certen hope of resurrection to eternall lyfe I do commyt my body unto the earth, the mother of all flech, willing the same to be buryed in the churchyade of hartest' (10).

The emphasis on personal salvation continued throughout the 17th century, and found its most eloquent expression in the testament of Thomas Wright, Gentleman, written in 1646, and who had founded the widows' almshouses in his lifetime. '. . . humbly, Joyfully, and willingly yeilding my soule into the hands of Almightie God my maker, and my body I comitt to the Earth whereof it was framed, knowing it must returne to its first principles soe to continue untill the general awkeinge day, when by the mightie power of my God I hope to reassume the same my body, which being then united to my soule againe, through the unspeakable mercies of my Lord and alone Savior Jesus Christe, shall I trust inheritt everlasting blessedness in the Kingdome of Heaven not for any meritts of myne (for I acknowledge my selfe the worst of all men), but for the most glorious meritts, bitter death and passion of my most gracious and mercifull Savior and Redeemer Jesus Christe, to whom be all glory and praise forever Amen . . .' (11).

Towards the end of the 17th century many of the testators merely commended their souls into the hands of 'God their Creator'. However, others continued with a full statement of faith. Robert Enos, a say weaver, in 1684 commended his soul in these words '. . . consideringe that it is appointed for all men once to dye that I may be in the greater redines to expect Gods good pleasuer I make this my last will & testament in manor & forme following principally I commend my mortall soule into the hands of God my Creator hopeinge by his mercies & the alsufficient merits of Jesus Christ my gratious Redeemer and the mighty opperations of the divine sanctifieing spirit to be fitted & brought to the enioyment of everlasting glory in hopes whereof I leave my body to be decently buried . . .' (12).

Thomas Cronshay in 1698 continued the familiar theme '. . . I commend my Soule into the hands of Almighty God hopeing through the meritts Death and passion of my Saviour Jesus Christ to have full and free pardon and forgiveness of all my sins and to inheritt Everlasting life . . .' (13).

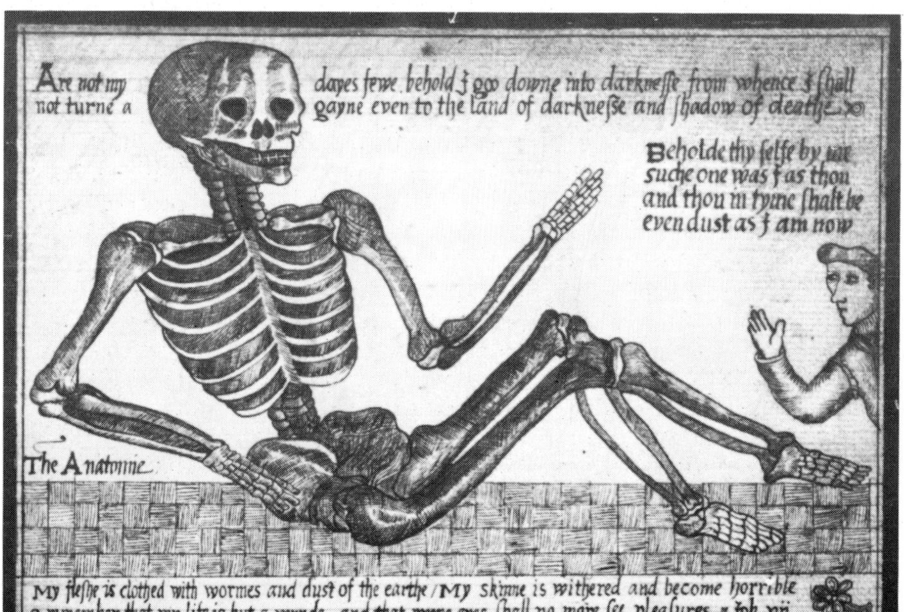

From a 'Book of Diverse Devices' by Thomas Fella of Dunwich (1585–1622).

The Fall of the Church Tower

A remarkable group of five documents from the Weller Poley and parish manuscripts gives a very detailed account of the events of 1650-52.

The first is a rare application, or petition, for a brief, which was usually a royal mandate giving permission for money to be collected within a defined area, towards a deserving cause. The details of the brief were read out by a Minister and the money collected after the service.

The Hartest petition (1), was authorised by the Court of Quarter Sessions at Bury St Edmunds on 20 January 1651. As Charles I had been executed two years earlier, the petition was addressed to Parliament as the '. . . supreame Authoritie of this nation'.

The document records that at 7 pm on Sunday 27 October 1650 the steeple, or tower, of the church collapsed and fell eastwards onto the nave and aisles '. . . by which fall a great part of the said church is beaten downe, and the rest much shaken . . .'. The total cost of the repairs was calculated to be £1,240, which they were unable to raise because of the poverty of the community.

As supporting evidence for the poverty of Hartest, interesting details are given about the number of families. All the 144 families are described as being 'exceeding poore', 100 of which were receiving poor relief, and the other 44 unable to pay any additional rates. Even allowing for some exaggeration by the petitioners the inhabitants were obviously unable to finance the cost of repairing the damage. The population in 1651, based on 144 families, can be estimated at between 620-650 individuals (2).

No evidence has been found to show how much money was collected as a result of the brief. However, it is likely that the repairs to the nave and aisles were either completed, or in hand, by 12 July 1652 when the contract for the tower repairs was signed (3).

Thomas Moore of East Bergholt agreed to '. . . bild the stepell up tenn foote above the church . . .' (that is above the height of the nave) and to '. . . make the frames and hang the bells'. The work was to be carried out between September 1652 and September 1653. The cost was to be £60 paid in four stages, £5 at the start, £15 when one third completed, £20 when two-thirds completed, and £20 as a final settlement.

The receipt for the first £5 was signed by Thomas Moore on 13 July 1652 (4). Two further documents (5) record the accounts submitted to 'Mr Teede', probably Ralph Tweed of Cooks Farm, who may also have been a churchwarden. These accounts give details of the wages to be paid to the labourers engaged on the work. They are undated, but show that Thomas Pawit, Obiet Write, Richard Risen, Andrew Shally and Thomas Cranshay have spent most of their money in advance. Thomas Moore requests Mr Teede '. . . to Paye it before Goody Hibbull, for they Owe most of the monyes to huer . . .'; perhaps she kept the local boarding or beer house.

BRIEF FOR REBUILDING HARTEST CHURCH TOWER

To the supreame Authoritie of this nation
the high and honroable Court of
Parliament

Whearas att a generall quarter Sessions of the peace holden att Bury St Edmunds the twentieth day of January Anno Domi 1650 (that is, 1651) by Edmund Harvey Esq, Gyles Barnardiston Esq, Gibson Lucas Esq, Sammuel Moody Esq, Thomas Chaplin Esq, John Clarke Esq, Justices of the peace of this County it appeared to this Court that on the seaven & twentieth day of October last past about seaven of the clocke in the after noone being the lords day the steeple of the Church of Hartest in the said County, fell uppon the body of the Church by which fall a great part of the said Church is beaten downe and the rest much shaken soe that the Inhabitants of the said towne are utterly destitute of a place of meeting for the worshippe and service of god. Which parish being exceeding poore, it consisting of seaven score and fower families whearof five score of them are receivers and the rest but meane inhabitants, And the costs and charge to rebuild the said Church and steeple will amount to twelve hundred and fourty pounds as by the oaths of severall workemen taken in Court doeth appeare, viz for Timber & Carriage and Carpenters worke fower hundred pounds for Iron worke fourty pounds for bricke & limbe and scaffolding stuff and all other materialls for the Masons and for theire worke seaven hundred pounds for glasse and leads and for Plummers and Glaciers worke one hundred pounds, All which considdered the said parishioners in regard of their extreame poverty are altogether unable to build or repair the same, The truth of this we whose names are here subscribed doe certifie to your honours and doe in the behalfe of the said parishioners humbly beseech your honours to grant your letters Pattents under the great seale of England that there may be such briefes sett out as may be for the collecting the charitable benevolence of all well disposed people within this Comonwealth, It being for soe charitable a worke

Edm: Harvey
Joseph Brand
Sam. Moody
Jo: Eden
Tho. Chaplin
G. Barnardiston
Robert Bacon
Gibson Lucas
John Clarke

SRO(B)FL557/5/2.

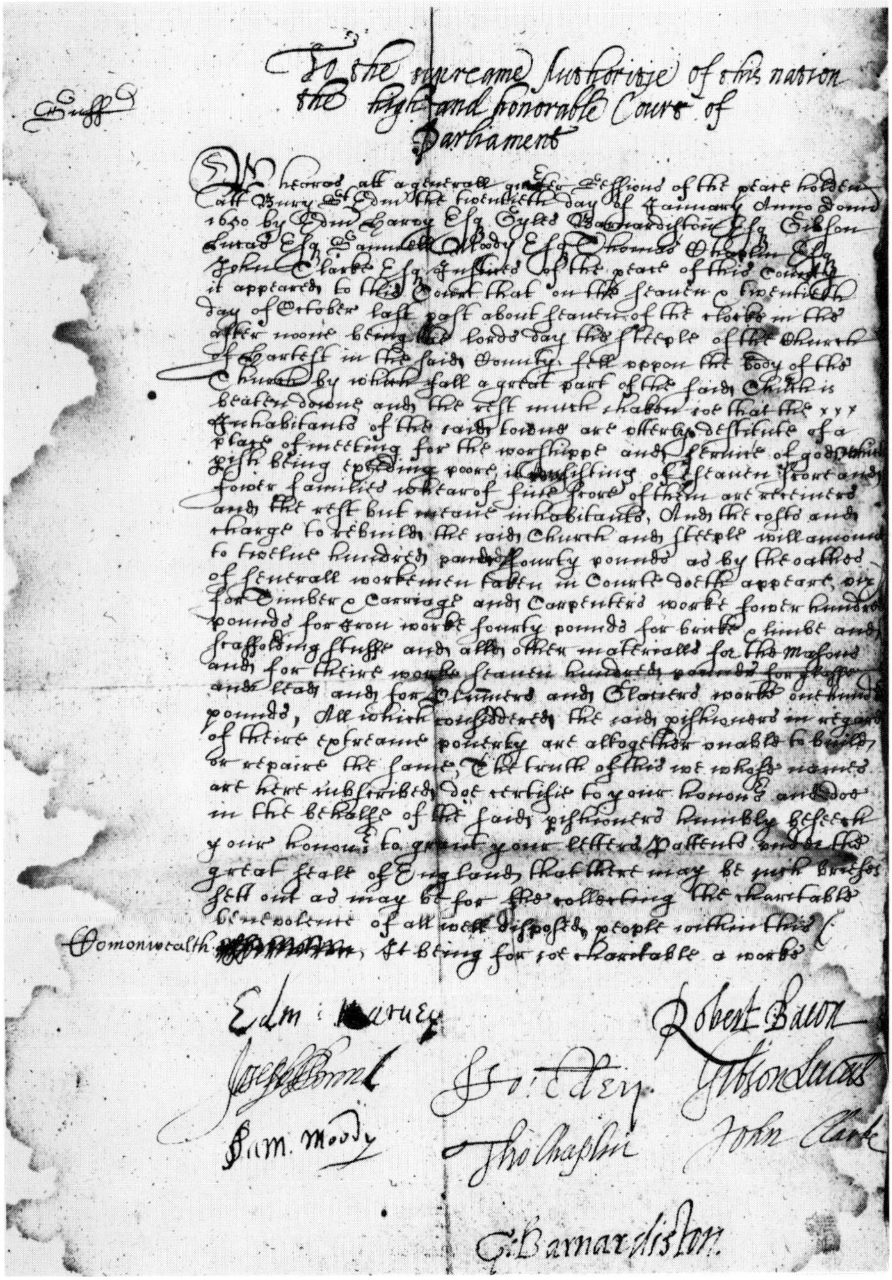

To the supreame Authoritye of this nation the high and honorable Court of Parliament

Suff

Wee whereas att a generall quarter Sessions of the peace holden att Bury St Edm the twentieth day of January Anno domi 1650 by Edm Harvy Esq Gyles Barnardiston Esq Gibson Lucas Esq Samuell Moody Esq Thomas Chaplin Esq John Clarke Esq Justices of the peace of this County it appeared to this Court that on the seaven & twentieth day of October last past about seaven of the clocke in the after noone being the lords day the steeple of the Church of Haverhill in the said County fell uppon the body of the Church by which fall a great part of the said Church is beaten downe and the rest much shaken soe that the xxx Inhabitants of the said towne are utterly destitute of a place of meeting for the worshipp and service of god which being exceeding poore consisting of seaven score and foure families whereof fiue score of them are releived and the rest but meane inhabitants. And the costs and charge to rebuild the said Church and steeple will amount to twelve hundreth pounds fourty pounds as by the oathes of severall workemen taken in Court doth appeare viz for Timber Carriage and Carpenters worke foure hundred pounds for Iron worke fourty pounds for bricke lime and scaffolding stuffe and all other materialls for the Masons and for their worke seaven hundreth pounds for glasse and lead and for Plumers and Glasiers worke one hundred pounds, All which considered the said petitioners in regard of their extreame poverty are altogether unable to build or repaire the same, The truth of this wee whose names are here subscribed doe certifie to your honours and doe in the behalfe of the said petitioners humbly beseech your honours to grant your letters Patents under the great seale of England that there may be such briefes sett out as may be for the collecting the charitable benevolence of all well disposed people within this Comonwealth, it being for soe charitable a worke

Edm: Harvey
Robert Bacon
Joseph Brond
Tho: Edey
Gibson Lucas
Sam. Moody
Tho Chaplin
John Clarke
G. Barnardiston

In common with many other 17th century church tower rebuildings red brick was used as the basic material. Other examples of brick towers locally are at Gislingham (1639), Drinkstone (1694) and Cowlinge (1733). At Hartest the belfry stage was rebuilt and battlemented and large buttresses erected to ensure that a similar disaster did not occur again.

The damage to the nave and aisles resulted in the lowering of the nave walls, by the removal of the clerestory windows; the rebuilding of the arcades on each side; and the construction of a nave roof with characteristic 17th century pendants. The roof was renewed again in the 1879 restoration and from its style must have been modelled on the earlier design.

A carpenter: from 'A Collection of Emblemes' by George Wither (1635).

Charities

John Poley

The oldest charity in Hartest is that established by John Poley of Boxted Hall in 1572. He bequeathed to trustees, lands in Burwell, Exning and Fornham All Saints, the rents from which were to be used for the poor people of Glemsford, Stanstead, Hartest, Somerton and Boxted. The sum of 13s. 4d. had to be distributed twice a year in each parish between St Andrew's Day (30 November) and Christmas Day, and between Lady Day (24 March) and Easter. Any surplus income was to be equally divided among the five parishes (1).

In 1844 the income enabled each parish to receive £8, in 1892 £11, and in 1912 £10 10s. In the late 19th century, coal was given instead of money at Hartest, and newly minted silver coins at Boxted.

The land belonging to the charity at Exning was sold in 1884, land at Fordham All Saints in 1895 and at Burwell in 1956. The income from investments was £35 in 1982 and £27 in 1983, which was distributed in amounts ranging from £2 to £3. Mrs P. Ward is the present Hartest trustee for the charity.

John Corder

In 1636 John Corder of Cockfield left land in Lawshall to provide money for the poor of Sudbury, Long Melford, Bury, Lawshall, Glemsford, Shimpling, Stanstead, Hartest, Cockfield, Alpheton and Stanningfield. The income was originally intended to buy bread for the poor during the first week of Lent. The Rector and churchwardens of Hartest were to receive £1 per annum for that purpose.

For some years the income has been used to buy coal. However, as the Hartest trustees still only receive £1 a year they are only able to purchase a bag every five years. The present trustees for Hartest are Mrs P. Ward and Mrs E. Clarke.

Thomas Wright

In 1646 Thomas Wright, gentleman, bequeathed two cottages to trustees '. . . for the benefitt and habitacion of two poore widowes . . . for soe longe as the world shall endure . . .' (2). The cottages were built as an encroachment on the road verge of Hartest Hill and today the site is marked by the former Brethren Chapel. Thomas described them as being '. . . upon which wayes (roads) two cottages for the habitation of two poore widdowes are newly by me erected and builded . . .'.

He laid down rules for the widows living in the cottages who were '. . . not to be such as have bene a charge or chargeable to the said parish of Hartest.

'Touching the placing of which sayd widows, I will that the instructions, articles and rules, in this my will and testament expressed, be duely and justly from time and for ever observed, vizt.

'1. That the same widdows and every of them shall constantly repaire to the church of Hartest aforesaid, at the times of all publique exercises of religion, and shall there behave themlselves orderly from the beginninge of such exercises untill the end thereof, without any excuse whatsoever to be admitted, saveing only sickness or decrepit age.

'2. That the same widowes and every of them shall receive the Eucharist twice at least in every yeare, (vizt.) once at or aboute the time of Easter, and once at or about the feast day of the birth of our Lord and Saviour Christe, if the same be soe often administered.

'3. That none of these widowes there to be placed shall be under the age of Fifty yeares at the time of such placeing there; and if they or any of them doe marry, then their place to be voyd, and such to be forthwith removed and displaced.

'4. That noe such widowe shall maintaine, keepe, or suffer any of her children, or any other person or persons whatsoeuer, to be resident, abide, or be sheltered there, saveing that it shall be lawfull for every widowe to have with her one of her owne daughters, being under the age of sixteene yeares and not above (if she shall have any such daughter), but if such daughter shall once have atteyned to the age of sixteene years, then shall such daughter be removed from her utterly; but in case of sicknes or other extreme necessitie every such widowe may have one to helpe her dureing that time.

'5. That every such widowe there to inhabite, shall be of good life, fame, and conversation, and shall live peacably and quietly without quarrelling or clamour.

'6. That noe such widowe nor any other person for them or any of them, or by their or any of their appointment, shall cutt, croppe, fell, have, or take any wood, underwood, trees or bushes, which are or shall be growing at any time hereafter in or upon the way or lane wherein the sayd almes house is erected, upon payne of removeall from thence utterly upon the first offence.

'7. And if any such widow or widowes shall offend in any of thaforesaid first five rules or articles herein mentioned, then they and every of them soe offendinge, after one admonition, shallbe forthwith displaced and put out of the sayd almes house by the foeffees or trustees thereof for the time being, and never afterwards to be restored againe.

'Item I will that the widow Walker, and the widow White, whom I haue placed in the said house, shall continue therein dureing their lives, they and either of them observeing the instructions, articles, and rules before menconed. Nevertheless my will and desire is that if any of myne, or either of my two wives linage or kindred, hereafter inhabiting in the said parish of Hartest, and being widowes or single women of the age of thirtie years or more, shall be in want and povertie, that then they or any of them shall from time to time be preferred to the said house and place before any other, yet subject to the rules, instructions, and articles before . . .'.

The two cottages were sold in 1869 for £18 which was invested, and the interest used for the care of four poor widows in their own homes. The original bequest included an annual rent charge of 10s. on part of Penns tenement, which with 11s. 8d. interest in 1895, gave the total income of £1 1s.8d.

The income in 1982 amounted to 52p. interest and 50p. rent charge, the total capital being only £24. The present trustees are the Rector and the Churchwardens of Hartest.

Thomas Sparke

In 1721 Thomas Sparke of Rougham, gentleman, whose family had lived in Hartest from the 1560s established a charity to provide schooling for poor children. He bequeathed a house and 40 acres of land (later known as Charity Farm) to trustees, for the '. . . buying of books and the schooling of poor children of and within the said parish of Hartest . . .' (3).

The Rectors of Hartest, Brockley and Rede were each to receive £1 a year from the income for examining the annual accounts; the poor children of Brockley were to have £6 a year spent on their education; the repairs and upkeep of the farmhouse and buildings were to be deducted, and the remainder spent on the education of the poor children of Hartest.

Income from the farm varied from £40 to £70 a year, according to the value of agricultural land in the 19th century. Between 1908 and 1925 the rent only brought in £24 each year, and the farm was eventually sold in the 1930s. The interest on the capital is still spent on the education of the children of Hartest. In recent years the Primary school has received donations towards the library, a climbing frame and a computer; the village play group has also received help towards tables and chairs for the children. The present trustees are the Rector and the Churchwardens of Hartest.

Bequests to the Poor

Many individuals, for pious or social reasons, bequeathed money, food, drink and fuel to the poor members of the community. Katherine Frost in 1539 gave '. . . to every poor householder within the town 4d and a peck of malt . . . and my wood in my yerde . . .' (4). Thomasyn Philipson (5) in 1570 left ten cheeses to the poor. John Haywood (6) in 1607 bequeathed 5s. a year to the poor for eight years following his death. Thomas Underwood, yeoman, in 1629 gave £1 '. . . to be paid to the Churchwardens and Overseers for the poore of Hartest . . . to be distributed amongst the most aged and needy poore . . .' (7). John Hall, yeoman, in 1628 ordered that £1 a year should be paid for five years to the Churchwardens and Overseers to be distributed '. . . upon the first day of January or upon the next Sunday following . . .' (8).

In the 1670s–1690s money was given to purchase bread for the poor, to be distributed over several Sundays. Richard Cranshay, gentleman, in 1685 gave £5 to the poor '. . . especially unto such as do most frequent their church and are most aged . . . in bread upon five first Lords days after my decease' (9). George Hibble, yeoman, in 1695 bequeathed £5 '. . . to be given out in bread by the Churchwardens and Overseas, to those poore people which take noe Collection of the parish (that is, do not receive any poor relief) the first Sunday in the first five months next after my decease . . .' (10).

AN HOMILY OF
Almes-deeds, and mercifulneſſe toward the poore, and needy.

OF all the manifold duties that Almighty GOD requireth of his faythfull ſervants the true Chriſtians, by the which he would that both his Name ſhould be glorified, and the certainety of their vocation declared, there is none that is eyther more acceptable unto him, or more profitable for them, then are the workes of mercy, and pity ſhewed upon the poore, which be afflicted with any kind of miſery. And yet this notwithſtanding (ſuch is the ſlothfull ſluggiſhneſſe of our dull nature, to that which is good, and godly) that we are almoſt in nothing more negligent, and leſſe carefull then we are therein. It is therefore a very neceſſary thing that GODS people ſhould awake their ſleepy minds, and conſider their duety on this behalfe. And meete it is, that all true Chriſtians ſhould deſirouſly ſeeke, and learne what GOD by his holy Word doth herein require of them: that firſt knowing their duty (whereof many by their ſlackneſſe ſeeme to be very ignorant) they may afterwards diligently endevour to performe the ſame. By the which both the godly charitable perſons may be encouraged to goe forwards, and continue in their mercifull deeds of almes-giving to the poore, and alſo ſuch as hitherto have eyther neglected, or contemned it, may yet now at length (when they ſhall heare how much it appertayneth to them) adviſedly conſider it, and vertuouſly apply themſelves thereunto.

From: The Book of Homilies, 1635 edition.

Boxted Tithe Agreement 1683

The payment of tithe to the Church was a source of contention between parishioners and the local clergy until the 1930s. The tithe, or one tenth of all crops and livestock, was either paid in kind, or in money towards the support of the parish clergy. The Rector, who could either be a cleric or a layman, had the 'great tithes' of corn, hay and wood and the vicar or curate had the 'small tithes' on everything else.

Numerous legal disputes arose over these payments. One such was in 1682 between the Rev William Butts, Rector of Hartest and Boxted, and the parishioners of Boxted over the payment of tithe on lactage or milk.

It seems that the Rector had tried to make the cattle owners of Boxted pay the tithe on milk in kind. They produced sworn statements from Bridgett Brown aged 83, John Pawsey aged 74 and Elizabeth Gault aged 78, which proved that a composition or modus for the payment of 4d. for each milk cow had been the custom since before 1616 (1). The Rev Humphrey Vero, Rector 1616-1627, and his successor Rev Frederick Gibb, Rector 1627-1644, had both accepted the payment in lieu of milk.

The evidence also shows the length to which individuals were prepared to go in order to collect or to avoid the tithe. Robert Pawsey sometime before 1622 had hired a farm in Boxted, but lived in Hartest. He milked his cows in Boxted and took the milk to Hartest in order to make cheese and butter. The Rector, Mr Vero, demanded payment in kind as the milk was being processed in Hartest where no modus had been agreed. Pawsey, in order to avoid the payment in kind, built a shed in a ditch in Boxted , adjoining his house in Hartest and made his cheese and butter there. Because he now milked his cows and processed the milk in Boxted, he paid the 4d. modus for each cow.

As a result of this evidence, the Rev Butts agreed to accept the cash payment for the tithe on milk, and also that if he took legal action over the matter, then the sworn statements could be used as evidence against him. For their part the parishioners agreed not to take legal action against him in the Court of Exchequer.

The agreement existed until 1839, when all the tithes in Boxted were commuted to an annual cash payment.

see over leaf for original documents

EVIDENCE ABOUT TITHES IN BOXTED

John Pawsey of Brockley in the County of Suffolk, yeoman, being of the age
of Seaventy & Four yeares or thereaboutes, & Elizabeth Gawlt of the same town, widdow,
being of the age of Seaventy & Eight yeares or thereaboutes, make
Oathe That one Robert Pawsey, Father to these deponents, Sixty yeares since and upwardes did
hire a Farme of William Gallant lying in Boxsted in the said
County (which Farme is since come to Sir John Pooly knight & his heires),
and other groundes lying in Boxsted aforesaid, and by reason
the howse belonging to the said William Gallants farme was then building,
these deponents said father did live in parte of his brother Thomas Pawsey
howse in Hartest in the said County, during which time these deponents said father
did milke all the Cowes he kept upon William Gallantes
farme, & the other groundes he hired lying in Boxsted, att Boxsted
and did bringe all the Milke of these Cowes to the parte of
the howse where he then lived in Hartest, and did there make Butter & Cheese thereof, by
reason whereof
one Mr Vero, the minister of Boxsted & Hartest, did demand
of these deponents said father tyth in kind for the same, and these
deponents said father acquainting the said Mr Vero that there was
a Custome in Boxsted aforesaid to pay Four pence a
Cowe in liewe & satisfaction of lacktage, whereupon Mr Vero did
reply, that by reason the the Milke was brought from Boxsted
aforesaid to Hartest aforesaid & the Butter & Cheese was made
there he the said Mr Vero did expect, that these deponents
said father should pay tythe in kind as the rest of the towne
of Hartest did, for although there was Custome in
Boxsted to pay Four pence a Cowe in liew of Lacktage, yett
there was noe such Custome in Hartest, And thereupon these
depondents said father did build upp a Shed in Walter Paines ditch
lying in Boxsted, neare that parte of the howse where he then lived in
Hartest, where he did make all the Butter & Cheese of the Milke
that his Cowes gave that were fed upon William Gallantes
Farme & the other grounds he hired in Boxsted, and then these deponents
said father payd to Mr Vero Four pence a Cowe and noe more in liew & satisfaction
for the tythe of Lacktage, which the said Mr Vero received accordingly

10 November 1682.

his
John [mark] Pawsey
marke

her
Elizabeth [mark] Gawlt
mark.

S.R.O.(B)HA519/585(b)

John Pawsey of Brockley in the County of Suff yeoman being of the age of seaventy & ffour yeares or thereabouts & Elizabeth Hawlt of the same towne wid being of the age of seaventy & eight yeares or thereabouts make oath That one Root Pawsey father to these deponts sixty yeares since and upwards did hire a ffarme of william Gallant lying in Boxsted in the sd county (wch ffarme is since come to Sr John Poly knight & his heires) and other grounds lying in Boxsted aforesd, and by reason the howse belonging to the sd willm Gallants farme was then building, these depont sd father did live in parte of his brother Thomas Pawseys howse in Hartest in the sd County, during wch time these depont sd father did milke all the cowes he kept upon willm Gallants farme & the other grounds he hired lying in Boxsted att Boxsted and did bring all the milke of those cowes to the parte of the howse where he then lived in Hartest and did there make Butter & Cheese thereof by reason whereof one mr Vere then minister of Boxsted & Hartest did demand of these depont sd father tythe in kind for the same and these depont sd father acquainting the sd mr Vere that there was a Custome in Boxsted aforesd to pay ffour pence a cowe in liew & satisfaction of lacktage, whereupon mr Vere did reply that by reason the Milke was brought from Boxsted aforesd to Hartest aforesd & the Butter & Cheese was made there he the sd mr Vere did expect, that these depont sd father should pay tythe in kind as the rest of the towne of Hartest did, for although there was a Custome in Boxsted to pay ffour pence a cowe in liew of lacktage, yett there was not such Custome in Hartest, and thereupon these depont sd father did build up a Shed in Walters Pannes ditch lying in Boxsted neare the gate of the howse where he then lived in Hartest, where he did make all the Butter & Cheese of the milke that his cowes gave that were fed upon willm Gallants farme & the other grounds he hired in Boxsted, and then these depont sd father payd to mr Vere ffour pence a cowe and noe more in liew & satisfaction for the tythe of lacktage, wch the sd mr Vere rec'd accordingly

Jur' apud Brockley in Com' Suff 8° die Nov. A° xxxxiiij° Car 2 di[illegible] Coram me

Tho: Hustler
in Canc' mr' Extr'

John his Pawsey mark

Elizabeth her Hawlt mark

Philippa Munnings: The Hartest Witch?

Philippa Munnings a widow, was accused and tried on four charges of witchcraft, at the Bury Assizes in January 1694.

The first charge was that on 10 February 1685 she had bewitched to death Thomas Pannel her landlord. The details presented to the Court were that Pannell wanted to evict Philippa from one of his houses, she had refused to leave and he then removed the door to the house. Some time later as he was passing by, Philippa threatened him, no doubt through the door frame, saying 'go thy way, thy nose shall lie upward in the churchyard before Sunday next'. This was nearly a true prophecy as he died on 1 March, having on his deathbed accused Philippa of causing his demise. The Court found her not guilty of the charge.

The Rev. Francis Hutchinson, Minister of St James, Bury St Edmunds, published the details of the case in his book 'An Historical Essay Concerning Witchcraft' in 1718. He made enquiries in Hartest and discovered that Thomas Pannel was '. . . a consumptive spent man and the words not exactly as they (the witnesses) had sworn them' (1). It is also interesting to note that the only record of a Thomas Pannell being buried in Hartest occurred in June 1677 and not 1685.

The second charge was that on 5 March 1688 she had bewitched to death James Parkin who died 1 April of the same year. He was in fact buried on 7 February 1685 and the Court decided there was no case to answer.

The third charge was that she did 'consult and covenant' with the devil, who gave her two evil spirits or imps in the likeness of polecats. Nine inhabitants of Hartest made the accusation, one of whom '. . . coming from the Alehouse about nine at night, he looked in at her window, and saw her take out of her basket two imps, a black and a white. Other witnesses, for the defence, swore that the white imp was a '. . . lock of wool taken out of the basket to spin and the black one its shadow.' (2). The Court found her not guilty, common sense outweighing fear, prejudice and the effects of the alehouse.

The last charge was that she had on 10 March 1692 bewitched to death Mary Drury, who had accused Philippa on her death bed, and died on 1 April. It is interesting to note that all those she bewitched died on the first of March or April. Again she was found not guilty and again there is no record of the burial in the parish register.

Why then was Philippa accused of these things? In the earlier period of witchcraft trials in the 1640s and 1660s the accusation was used to settle old scores and to find a scapegoat for disaster and deaths that the community did not understand. She was also supposedly responsible for turning beer sour and injuring cattle; Sarah Wager was struck dumb and lame after a quarrel with her; and a local doctor said she was '. . . a dangerous woman, she could touch the line of life . . .' (3).

Philippa continued to live in Hartest after the trial. Hutchinson records that she declared her innocence until the day of her death. Her burial at least is recorded in the parish register '. . . The Widow Mundings Buryed Dec 9 1696' (4).

John Frost: The Tanner

John Frost, who died in 1661, is the only recorded tanner in Hartest in the 17th century. He lived at a house called 'Warrens' with six acres of land, which does not seem to have been on the site of the house of the same name today. A description of the abuttals shows it stood on the east side of the road from Cross Green towards Brockley. Could this be the land and house belonging to the present Tan Office Farm?

His inventory gives details of the equipment connected with his trade (1). He had bark in the barns estimated at 'about 16 loads . . . the things and goods belonging to the tan yard, 69 backes, 76 hides, 9 bullock skines, 32 calves skinnes, the bark mill (for grinding the bark) and other things belonging thereto . . .' all amounting to £141 1s. 0d. or 40% of his total wealth.

Like many of the land holding members of society John also engaged in agriculture in addition to his trade. He had cheese, butter, sacks, a bushell, a fan and wool, stored within the house. In the barn were '. . . 12 Jaggs of hay with a parcell of wheat and barley and a little bullingmong abroad (in the field) . . .' and corn from last year's harvest. There were also 6 cowes, two bullocks, a nag, a mare, 17 sheep and lambs, two hogs, an old cart, two collars, a plough, a pair of harrows and hop poles. This section of his inventory amounted to £63 10s. 0d. or 17.9% of the total valuation.

His household goods were valued at £67 2s. 0d. or 18.7% of the total. These items included 6 beds, two framed tables; 6 joined or jointed stools, three cupboards, one of which was glass fronted; a child's cradle, 24 pieces of pewter on three shelves; a flagon; two silver spoons; household linen, cooking, brewing and dairying utensils.

His debts and ready money came to £81 10s. 0d. or 23% of his total wealth. At the time of making his will in August 1661, John made bequests to his wife Ann, his sons John, Thomas and Samuel and his daughters Bridget, Dorothy and Elizabeth. Unusually both will and inventory list the items given to his wife, who was to have '. . . one posted bedstead standing in the pantry chamber, with the featherbed (mattress) to bowlster, too pillows, one coverlet, one blanket, one payer of hollon sheets, three pillowberes (pillowcases) of hollon, to payer of new hempen shettes, with the Curtanes & curtane rodes about the bed, a hutch (chest) which was my fathers, and a new red bearing cloth (christening robe) with blew ribbing about it, one white blanket and all the child bed linnen, three pewter Dyshes marked with M & C, one flagon, one porringer (an earthenware porridge bowl with lid and handle), to silver spoons, one cradle, to pillows, one back chayre, one tubb which was my brothers, her best hat and a new quart skillet (pot with short legs for setting in the fire)'.

His son John was to have the house and land called 'Warrens', a house in Boxted, and all the rest of his movable goods. Each of the other five children were to receive £20 when they were 21 years old.

John Frost was a wealthy member of the community, his valuation at £353 3s. ranking with that of Thomas Cranshay, gentleman who in 1664 was worth £371 11s. 2d. Hartest obviously had the necessary supply of hides and bark readily available for the tanning trade. It may be that the great and little woods were coppiced to help maintain the supply of bark.

Gathering wood: from 'A Book of Diverse Devices' by Thomas Fella of Dunwich (1585-1622).

Two Hartest Shopkeepers

Many household items, spices, various types of cloth and haberdashery goods could not be produced locally, and had to be purchased from the village grocer. Details of two such shops and their contents have survived from 1670 and 1720.

Andrew Byatt in his will (1) of 1666 described himself as a 'Gentleman' but those men making an inventory (2) of his goods in 1670, including his sons-in-law, described him as a 'Grocer'. They no doubt give us a more accurate indication of his social position as seen by the rest of the community.

Details contained in the will show that he owned, or leased, several properties in Suffolk and Norfolk. In Hartest he owned a house and land called 'Smyths' situated adjacent to the road to Stanstead; and other houses and lands not specified, but including the house and shop. Other properties were a house and land in Bury St Edmunds, Long Melford, Sudbury, Great Yarmouth and Thetford. Some of them were bequeathed to relatives and the rest sold in order to pay legacies amounting to £565. The value of his goods and chattels contained in the inventory came to £332 3s. 7d. of which £157 19s. 1d. or 47% represented the stock in the shop.

The shop contained mainly drapery and haberdashery goods. The lengths of cloth are described as 'parcelles, peeces or remnants' and the weight or number of other items not stated, therefore no unit prices can be established.

The wool based cloths available were, Red Cheyney or 'Chany'; Searge, a very durable cloth used mainly for clothing; Kersey, originally taking its name from the Suffolk village, a coarse narrow cloth usually ribbed; Broadcloth, a fine double width cloth used mainly for clothing; Linsey Woolsey, a cloth made from a mixture of wool and flax; several parcells of wool, described as 'laine' a corruption of the latin for wool; and several items of 'Stuff' a general term for light worsted fabrics.

Cotton based cloths in stock were white and coloured Calico; Ticking or 'Tekens', a strong hard material used for making pillow and mattress cases; and Red Cotton. Cloths made from flax or hemp were Canvas, a strong coarse unbleached cloth; Lockrum, Holland and Hempen cloth. Finer materials were silk and blue linings.

Haberdashery items comprised Silk ribbons; Galloons, a narrow close woven ribbon or braid of gold, silver or silk thread used for trimming clothes; Gimp lace, which derived its name from the 'gimp' or thicker thread used to form a raised pattern; loop lace, which could be either a trimming consisting of a series of loops, or a patterned lace with a fine net background; Silk lace; Worsted lace; buttons made or covered with silk and gimp; neck buttons and other items collectively described as 'Haberdashe Goods'.

There were also ready made clothes including Stockings, waistcoats, 'bodies' or bodices for dresses and 'made lyning'.

Hardware items were candles, soap, nails and 'ware' a collective term for

A true and Perfect Inventory of all and singular the Goods, Chattles, Rights and Credites of Andrew Byatt late of Hartest, in the County of Suffolk, Grocer, deceased, taken and Appraised by Richard Skynner gent, John Cawston gent, John Ray Mercer, and John Hayward yeoman, the Ninth day of September 1670. as Followeth.

In the Shopp	£.	s.	d.
Imprimis two peices of Red Chany at £2 16s. and one other peece of Chany at 14s.8d. in all	3	10	8
Item for several parcelles and Remnants of Stuffe at	9	5	4
Item for divers parcelles of Searge at	2	14	0
Item for several parcells of Coloured Callico, at £5 19s.3d. and several parcells of white Callico at £3 10s.6d. in all	9	9	9
Item for Linsey Woolseyes at	4	11	0
Item for one peece of Red Cotten at £1 3s.3d. and several peeces of Kerseys at £8 12s.10d. in all	9	16	1
Item for broad Cloaths at	24	15	0
Item for several Remnants of Lockrums at	3	0	10
Item for blue Lyninge at	1	11	5
Item for Hambros at	2	19	4
Item for Hempen Cloath, at	5	15	9
Item for Hollands at	2	11	9
Item for Canvas at	1	9	8
Item more for Divers parcells of Lyning Cloath	7	12	3
Item Silke Ribbones gallouns Loope Lace at	13	19	4
Item for Necke buttons at	0	3	0
Item for Silke Lace and Gimpe Lace at	5	0	0
Item for several parcells of worsted Lace at	1	0	0
Item for Silke and Gimpe buttons, at	1	4	0
Item for severall parcells of Laine at	2	5	4
Item for several sorts of bodies at	3	13	2
Item for Tekens at	0	12	0
Item for Stockens and Wascoates, at	4	4	4
Item for Haberdashe Goods at	5	11	11
Item for Silke	2	5	0
Item for Mace Aniseed Sope cinemon & Nailes	3	18	0
Item for browne paper, tobackco, some ode peeces of made Lyning, Schooles, waites, Measures, 2 Counters and White Starch at	2	11	0
Item for tare oyle, Lead, schooles, Beame and potts at	4	6	4
Item for Hampers, basketts, old tubs, Pully and an Iron Morter at	0	16	0
Item for severall parcells of Ware, Candle, Strong Water at	7	8	7
Item for Nutmegs and pepper at	3	12	4
Item for Suger, fine an corse at	5	7	3
Item for 28 lb. of blue pouder at 8d. per lb.	0	18	8

SRO(B):IC500/3/15/90.

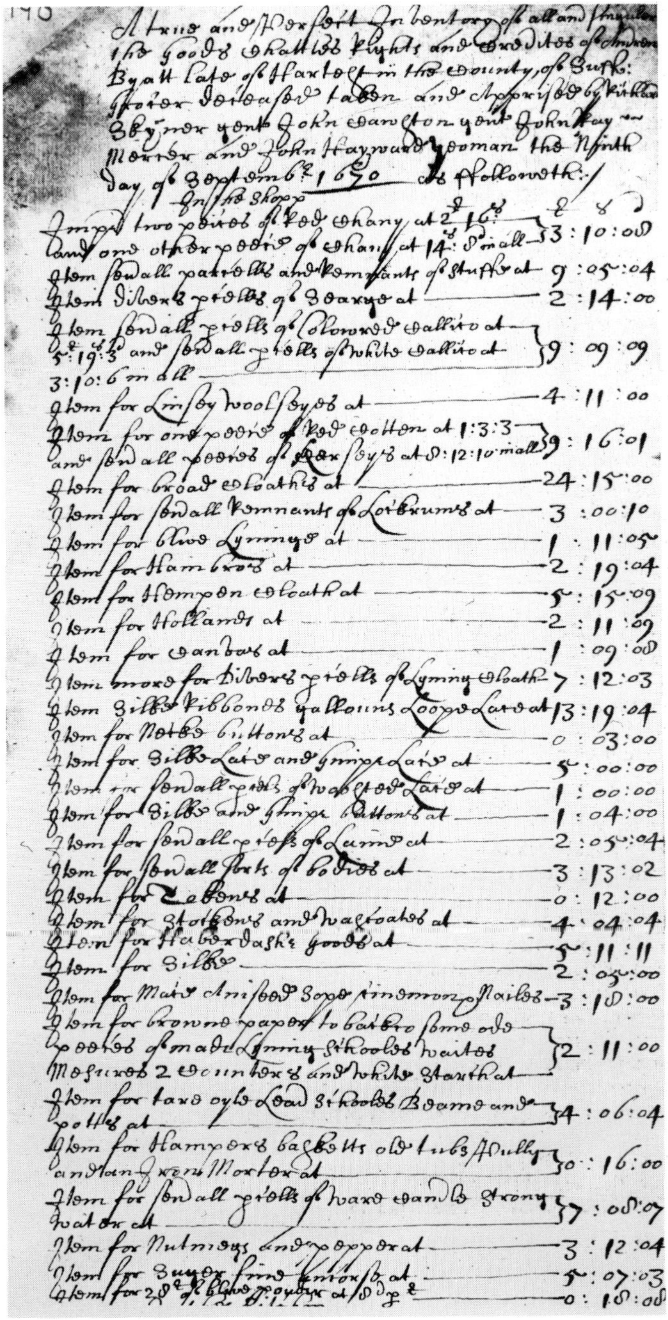

148

A true and Perfect Inventory of all and singular the Goods Chattles Rights and Credites of Andrew Byatt late of Harlest in the County of Suff: Grocer deceased taken and Apprised by Richard Skynner gent John Carlton gent John Kay Mercer and John Hayward yeoman the Ninth day of September 1670 as followeth:

In the Shopp

	£	s	d
Impris two peices of Red Chany at 2li 16s and one other peece of Chany at 14s: 8d in all	3	10	00
Item severall parcells and Remnants of Stuffe at	9	05	04
Item divers peices of Searge at	2	14	00
Item severall peices of Coloured Callico at 5li: 19s: 3d and severall peices of White Callico at 3: 10: 6 in all	9	09	09
Item for Linsey woolseys at	4	11	00
Item for one peece of Red Cotton at 1: 3: 3 and severall peeces of Kersey at 8: 12: 10 in all	9	16	01
Item for broad Cloathes at	24	15	00
Item for severall Remnants of [illegible] at	3	00	10
Item for blue Lynnings at	1	11	05
Item for Hamborg at	2	19	04
Item for Hempen Cloath at	5	15	09
Item for Hollands at	2	11	09
Item for Canvas at	1	09	08
Item more for divers peices of Lynnig Cloath	7	12	03
Item Silke ribbonds galloones Loope Lace at	13	19	04
Item for [illegible] buttons at	0	03	00
Item for Silke Lace and Gimpe Lace at	5	00	00
Item for severall peices of [illegible] Lace at	1	00	00
Item for Silke and Gimpe buttons at	1	04	00
Item for severall peices of Lawne at	2	05	04
Item for severall sorts of bodies at	3	13	02
Item for [illegible] at	0	12	00
Item for Stockens and wastcoates at	4	04	04
Item for Haberdash[er]s goods at	5	11	11
Item for Silke	2	05	00
Item for Mace Aniseed Sope tinder box [illegible] Nailes	3	18	00
Item for browne paper tobacco some odd peeces of made Lynnig Scales weites Measures 2 Counters and white Starch at	2	11	00
Item for tare oyle Lead Scales Beame and potts at	4	06	04
Item for Hampers baskets old tubs [illegible] and a [illegible] Morter at	0	16	00
Item for severall peices of ware candle strong water at	7	08	07
Item for Nutmegs and pepper at	3	12	04
Item for Sugar [illegible] at	5	07	03
Item for 28li of blue powder at 8d p li	0	18	08

earthenware. Washing or dyeing ingredients were blue powder at 8d. per pound and white starch.

There was a total absence of any meat, bread or perishable foodstuffs in the shop. Most households had their own cheese, butter and breadmaking equipment, and John Nelson a butcher had a house and shop abutting on the north side of 'Hunters' in 1670. However, scarcer or imported goods were available such as mace, aniseed, cinnamon, nutmeg, pepper and both fine and coarse sugar.

Tobacco and strong water (alcohol) were also on sale, but no indication of value or quantity given.

The shop goods and fittings were two counters with scales and weights, a larger pair of 'beam' scales with lead weights, various measures including pots, hampers, baskets and tubs; and 'tare oyle' which was either a container for weighing oil, or a type of tar oil; a pully; and an iron mortar, presumably for pounding some of the herbs.

Some fifty years later in 1720 the inventory of Thomas Orbell, a grocer was made (1). He died intestate and so we have no details of his real or personal estate other than those contained in the inventory. His goods and chattels amounted to £149 13s. 4d. of which £106 17s. 4d. or 71% was the contents of the shop.

The inventory was taken by John Gent a draper from Sudbury and William Boston a grocer from Long Melford. They gave a very detailed valuation of the stock, and with their working knowledge have provided us with an accurate account of contemporary prices.

The analysis of the contents of the shop will follow the pattern of the earlier inventory. Many of the items are common to both shops and technical descriptions will be given to those items found only in this shop. All prices have been converted to cost per yard unless otherwise indicated.

Wool based materials again formed the bulk of fabrics available, and the range had considerably increased. Broad cloth was priced at between 7s. and 11s. a yard; Narrow (Narr) cloth at between 3s. and 4s. 9d.; Narrow Green Cloth 4s.; Drugget, a thin narrow material, sometimes made of wool and silk, at between 1s. 2d. and 2s.; Sagathy, a type of serge, sometimes made of wool and silk, at between 1s. 6d. and 1s. 9d.; Duroy, a coarse West Country material 1s. 3d.; Serge, 1s. 6d.; Cloth Serge, between 1s. 8d. and 2s.; Shalloon 1s.; Flannelette, a very soft material twenty-eight inches wide; Calamanco, a glossy material extensively manufactured in Norwich, at between 11d. and 1s. 4d.; Worsted Rib, 1s.; Barragan, which was either a coarse waterproof cloth, or a fine silk cloth, 1s. 4d.; Poplin, a corded material made from wool and silk, 1s. 6d.; Flannel, an open material with a loose texture, 1s. 4d.; and various forms of 'stuff' at between 6d. and 11d. a yard.

Cotton based materials included Cotton itself at 6d.; Check Cotton 1s. 3d.; Pillow Ticking between 8d. and 11d.; Striped Ticking 1s.; a bed cover 11s.; Fustian, a coarse cloth made from cotton and flax 1s. 1d.; Calico between 2s. 3d. and 2s. 6d.; Muslin, a delicately woven fabric used for dresses, curtains and hangings; Camleteen or 'Camblettees' a cloth made from a mixture of cotton and linen, 1s. 5d.

Linen materials were far more extensive than in the earlier inventory and included Cheese cloth sold in two widths, as ell wide (45 inches) 1s. 2d., and eighteen inches wide 10d.; Holland cloth 3s. 2d.; Dowlas, a coarse linen 11d.; Printed linen 1s. 6d., check linen, blue linen and dyed linen all 9d.; blue and white linen 8d.; Black Damask and yard wide Damask both 1s.; Scotch cloth, a linen made from nettle fibres was available as yard wide 11d., and striped 1s. 4d.

Hemp cloth cost 10½d.; yard wide 11d. and ell wide between 1s. 3d. and 1s. 6d.; Rusha cloth cost 3d. and may have been a form of 'rushy cloth' a coarse hemp or flax based material.

Silks were represented by Canton Silk or 'Canting'; Striped Silk; Half Silk 1s.; and Striped and Rib Mantua.

Haberdashery goods were minutely itemised and comprised, pins at 1s. 6d. (? a packet) silver lace, between 10d. and 1s. a yard; various types of thread, including striped pack thread for sewing or tying up packs or bundles; blue thread at 2s. 10d. a pound; Lemon culled thread and brown culled thread at 1s. 8d. a pound; Nuns thread for very fine work; and unspecified types of thread at between 1s. 8d. and 3s. 6d. a pound; various tapes; lace and ribbons including Holland and narrow holland tape; Manchester binding; silk laces at 1s. 9d. a dozen; ribbons; Galloons; staybraids for drawing together stays or bodices; buttons included some covered with white thread and others that may have been covered with mohair; webbing cost 1s. 6d.; white crape 7d.; and 'cards' at 2s. a dozen. These could either have been plain cards in the modern sense, or carding combs for use with wool.

A wide range of ready made clothes were available. Cravats at 10d. each; caps 9d.; bonnets 4d.; gloves; silk handkerchiefs at between 1s. 2d. and 2s. 3d.; Gauze handkerchiefs 1s. 4d.; linen handkerchiefs 8d.; stockings for men 2s. 6d. a pair, women and girls' 1s. 2d., lads' 6d., girls' 4d. and childrens' 4d.; silk clocket stockings were the most expensive at 3s. a pair, 'clocket' meant that they had an ornamental pattern in silk on the side.

There were also two pieces of Mantuas at £1 2s. each. This may simply mean mantua silk, or possibly the loose fitting upper part of a dress or mantua.

Hardware goods included candles at £1 10s. a half hundredweight; soap and brick soap at 5d. a pound; corks; flag brooms at 3d. each; various dyes and colourings, whitening at 9d. a half hundredweight, bluing, indigo and stone blue all at 9d. a pound; and a pair of bellows at 6d. This item may have been part of his household effects and not part of the stock.

Foodstuffs were fewer than in the earlier inventory; sugar cost between 3d. and 5d. a pound; also available were salt, butter and bread. Tobacco was stored in the warehouse and valued at 11d. a pound.

Children's books were on sale in the form of horn books at ¾d. each, and primers at 2d. The former was a sheet of paper with the alphabet, numerals, Lord's Prayer and simple words printed or written on it, mounted on a tablet

A True & Perfect Inventory of all & Singular the Goods & Chattles of Thomas Orbell Grocer late of Hartest in the County of Suff. deceased. Taken & Apprized by us John Gent of Sudbury in the County Afforesaid Draper & William Boston of Melford Grocer in the said County of Suff. On the Thirteenth Day of December Anno Dom 1720 and are as followeth (that is to Say)

Imprimis. In ye Shop.

		£ s d
3 yds bro(ad) Cloth	at 7/–	1– 1–0
2 yds ¾ Do	at 7/–	0–19–3
2 yds Do	at 11/–	1– 2–0
1 yds ¾ Do	at 10/–	0–17–6
2 yds ½ Do	at 7/–	0–17–6
15 yds Narr(ow) Do	at 3/–	2– 5–0
14 yds Do	at 3/10	2– 5–0
5 yds Do	at 4/9	1– 3–9
2 yds Do	at 4/6	0– 9–0
2 yds Do	at 4/6	0– 9–0
1 yd Do	at 4/6	0– 4–6
17 yds Druggatt	at 1/10	1–11–2
7 yds Do	at 16d	0– 9–4
3 yds Do	at 16d	0– 4–0
2 yds Do	at 20d	0– 3–4
4 yds Do	at 22d	0– 7–4
4 yds Do	at 2/–	0– 8–0
12 yds Sagathy	at 18d	0–18–0
4 yds Do	at 21d	0– 7–0
3 yds Duroy	at 15d	0– 3–9
2 yds Serge	at 18d	0– 3–0
2 yds Cloth Serge	at 2/–	0– 4–0
4 yds Do	at 20d	0– 6–8
4 yds Shallon	at 12d	0– 4–0
1 yd Do	at 12d	0– 1–0
1 yd Cotton	at 6d	0– 0–6
4 yds ¾ Narr(ow) Green Cloth	at 4/–	0–19–0
4 yds ½ Druggat	at 14d	0– 5–3
A Bed Ticking	at 11/–	0–11–0
2 Remnants of fflannel	at 2/4	0– 2–4
14 yds Pillow Ticking	at 8d	0– 9–4
13 yds Do	at 12d	0–13–0
8 yds Calamanco	at 16d	0–10–8
4 yds Webben	at 18d	0– 6–0
A Percell of Damaged Gloves	at	0–15–0
1 doz ½ pins	at	0–12–0
		22–17–0

		£ s d
Remnats of Lace	at	0– 1– 0
A percel of ffootings	at	0– 1– 0
A percel of pins	at	0– 2– 0
5 yds ½ waste Rib	at 12d	0– 5– 6
3 yds Barragen	at 16d	0– 4– 0
9 yds Strip Ticking	at 12d	0– 9– 0
11 yds ffustian	at 13d	0–11–11
11 yds Do	at 9d	0– 7– 6
7 yds Strip'd pack thread	at 12d	0– 7– 0
15 yds Rusha Cloth	at 3d	0– 3– 9
8 yds of Ell-wide cheese Cloth	at	0– 9– 4
Remnants of Wosted	at	0– 5– 4
16 Ells ¾ Hambro	at 8d	0–11– 2
4 yds Holland	at 3/2	0–12– 8
1 yd ½ Do	at 15d	0– 1–10½
21 yds Dowlace	at 11d	0–19– 3
6 yds ¾ Callico	at 2/6	0–15– 7½
4 yds ¼ Do	at 2/3	0– 9– 6¾
3 yds ½ Printed Linen	at 18d	0– 5– 3
2 Cravats	at	0– 1 8
2 yds ¼ Stiped Scotch-cloth	at 18d	0– 3– 0
A Remnant of Canting	at	0– 1– 8
10 yds of Yd:wide Scotch cloth		0– 9– 2
7 yds ¾ Do	at 11d	0– 7– 1
Remnants of Muslins	at	0–10– 0
5 Caps	at 9d	0– 3– 9
15 yds himpen Cloth	at 10½d	0–13– 1½
5 Silk handkercheifs	at 2/3	0–11– 3
5 Do	at 14d	0– 5–10
10 Gorse Do	at 16d	0–13– 4
16 Linen Do	at 8d	0–10– 8
19 yds ½ Cotton Check	at 15d	1– 4– 4
5 yds blue & white linen	at 8d	0– 3– 4
2 yds ¾ Linen Check	at 9d	0– 2– 0¾
2 yds ½ blue Linen	at 9d	0– 1–10½
2 yds ¼ Dy'd Do	at 9d	0– 1– 8
4 yds ½ yd wide Cheese cloth		0– 3– 9
		13–10– 0

SRO(B):IC500/3/30/74

Tenn Pence per Quire

A True & Perfect Inventory of all & Singular the Goods & Chattles of Thomas Orboll, Grocer late of Hartest in the County of Suffc deceased, taken & Apprized by us John Gent of Sudbury in the County afforesaid Grocer & William Boston of Melford Grocer in the said County of Suffc. On the thirteenth day of Decembr Anno Dom 1720 and are as followeth (that is to say)

Imprimis. In ye Shop

		£ s d
3 yds bro Cloth	at 7/	1:1:0
2 yds ¾ Do	at 7/	0:19:3
2 yds Do	at 11/	1:2:0
1 yds ¾ Do	at 10/	0:17:6
2 yds ½ Do	at 7/	0:17:6
15 yds Narr Do	at 3/	2:5:0
14 yds Do	at 3/10	2:13:8
5 yds Do	at 4/9	1:3:9
2 yds Do	at 4/6	0:9:0
2 yds Do	at 4/6	0:9:0
1 yd Do	at 4/6	0:4:6
17 yds Druggat	at 1/10	1:11:2
7 yds Do	at 16d	0:9:4
3 yds Do	at 16d	0:4:0
2 yds Do	at 20d	0:3:4
4 yds Do	at 22d	0:7:4
4 yds Do	at 2/	0:8:0
12 yds Sagathy	at 18d	0:18:0
4 yds Do	at 21d	0:7:0
3 yds Duroy	at 15d	0:3:9
2 yds Serge	at 18d	0:3:0
2 yds Cloth Serge	at 2/	0:4:0
4 yds Do	at 20d	0:6:8
4 yds Shalloon	at 12d	0:4:0
1 yd Do	at 12d	0:1:0
1 yd Cotton	at 6d	0:0:6
4 yds ¾ Narr Green Cloth	at 4/	0:19:0
4 yds ½ Druggat	at 14d	0:5:3
A Bed Ticking	at 11/	0:11:0
2 Remnants of fflannel	at 2/4	0:2:4
14 yds Pillow Ticking	at 8d	0:9:4
13 yds Do	at 12d	0:13:0
8 yds Calamanco	at 16d	0:10:8
4 yds Webbon	at 18d	0:6:0
A Porcell of Damaged Gloves	at	0:19:0
1 doz ½ pins	at	0:12:0
		22:17:0

		£ s d
Remnats of Lace	at	0:1:0
A parcel of ffootings	at	0:1:0
A parcel of pins	at	0:2:0
5 yds ½ wosted Rib	at 12d	0:5:6
3 yds Barragon	at 16d	0:4:0
9 yds Stript Ticking	at 12d	0:9:0
11 yds ffustion	at 13d	0:11:11
10 yds Do	at 9d	0:7:6
7 yds Striped pack thread	at 12d	0:7:0
15 yds Ruska Cloth	at 3d	0:3:9
8 yds of Ell-wide Chess-cloth	at	0:9:4
Remnants of Wosted	at	0:5:0
16 Ells ¾ Hambro	at 8d	0:11:2
4 yds Holland	at 3/2	0:12:8
1 yd ½ Do	at 15d	0:1:10½
21 yds Dowlace	at 11d	0:19:3
6 yds ¼ Callico	at 2/6	0:15:7½
4 yds ¼ Do	at 2/3	0:9:6¾
3 yds ½ Printed Linen	at 18d	0:5:3
2 Cravats	at	0:1:8
2 yds ¼ Striped Scotchcloth at 16d		0:3:0
A Remnant of Canting	at	0:1:8
10 yds of yd: wide Scotch cloth		0:9:2
7 yds ¾ Do	at 11d	0:7:1
Remnants of Muslins	at	0:10:0
5 Caps	at 9d	0:3:9
15 yds Kimpon Cloth	at 10d½	0:13:1½
5 Silk handkerchiefs	at 2/3	0:11:3
5 Do	at 14d	0:5:10
10 Gorse Do	at 16d	0:13:4
16 Linen Do	at 8d	0:10:8
19 yds ½ Cotton Check	at 15d	1:4:4½
5 yds blue & white Linen	at 8d	0:3:4
2 yds ¾ Linen Check	at 9d	0:2:0¾
2 yds ½ blue Linen	at 9d	0:1:10½
2 yds ¼ Dyd Do	at 9d	0:1:8
4 yds ½ yd wide Chess cloth		0:3:9
		13:10:0

of wood, with a handle and covered with a thin sheet of transparent horn. The Primer was an elementary reading book.

The shop fittings were less well detailed and only the scales, weights, mortar and pestle in the shop, and the 'great scales and beam' in the warehouse were recorded.

Boxted Hall c.1800, the Weller Poley family have occupied a house on this site since the late 14th century.

The Weller Poley Family

The Poley, and later the Weller Poley, family have lived at Boxted Hall from the late 14th century until the present day. The 600 year connection began in the reign of Richard II (1377-99), when Thomas Poley of Codreth, Hertfordshire, married Ann the daughter and heir of Thomas Badwell, Lord of Boxted Manor. Their son, Thomas became heir of the Boxted estate and died in 1461. His son and heir John inherited the manor of Wormingford in Essex and died in 1487. Richard Poley (1468-1547) was buried at Boxted and a small brass plate in the chancel marks his grave.

John Poley (1500-1580) in 1572 established the Poley charity for the poor of the surrounding parishes (see section on charities). In 1561 he leased the hall and manor to his son William although he continued to have '. . . the parlowre at the end of the hall at the Scite of the said manor with the chamber within the same parlower. And also Stablinge for two Geldings at the said Scite in the stable at the end of the berne . . . and . . . the pleasure and libtie of the fisshe and fisshinge of the Moote Ryver and other waters . . .' (1).

The description of the hall with a parlour at one end, fits the plan of the building today, the parlour being either the present dining or drawing room. This gives us evidence that parts of the building date from at least the 1560s.

William eventually inherited the manor in 1580 on the death of his father. In 1540 he had married Alice Shae of Horndon-on-the-Hill, Essex and thus that manor was also acquired by the family. Both William (d.1587) and Alice (d.1577) have rare oak effigies over their altar tomb in Boxted Church. He is dressed in armour, with his head resting on a helmet, she has a pillow inscribed 'Blessed are the dead who die in the Lord A.P.1579, Mar 7'. There is a discrepancy between the date on the monument and that recorded in the parish register, which gives her burial as 7 March 1577.

Their son and heir Sir John Poley (1557-1590) served for 15 years as a Captain of Lancers in the Netherlands, under the command of the Earl of Leicester and Lord Willoughby. He was knighted after the siege of Bergen in 1588 and died in Flanders in 1590 or 1593. A large painting of a grey charger at Boxted is, according to family tradition, the horse of Sir John, which after his death, returned unaided to Boxted.

The estate then passed to his brother Sir William Poley (1562-1629) who had been knighted at Cadiz in 1596 by the Earl of Essex. He was M.P. for Sudbury in 1623 and 1628.

A cousin of both Sir John and Sir William, was Sir John Poley (1558-1638) of Wormegay in Norfolk. In 1636 he wrote a summary of his own career and a brief family history in order to prove the right of the Poleys to have a black lion rampant as their crest. From this document (2) we learn he served three years as a Captain of English footsoldiers under Henry IV of France, and in 1603 he was Colonel General of 4,000 footsoldiers, and for 22 years served King Christian of Denmark. There are alabaster monuments to both Sir John and his wife Abigail (d.1652) in the Poley chapel. He is described as 'a man famous for his bravery in arms and for military skills to be reckoned amongst the first commanders'. Both the effigies were erected long after their deaths, Sir John's is late 17th century, and supposedly the work of Bushnell; Dame Abigail's dates from 1725 and is believed to be the last English monument made of alabaster (3).

Sir John has a golden frog earring, the explanation for which has baffled, and will probably continue to baffle, historians for generations. The explanations suggested are, firstly the name Poley is derived from the Suffolk word 'Pollywiggle' meaning a tadpole; secondly the frog is both a lively and a cool animal, qualities which are essential in a soldier; thirdly, it is part of the insignia of the Danish Order of the Elephant, which was disproved by the Rev. Coppinger-Hill in the 1930s (4). We will probably never know the true explanation, although Sir John Cullum seems to have solved the mystery leaving us this cryptic comment '. . . The reason for wearing the frog earring is very simple and is cleared up in . . .' (5).

Sir William Poley (1602-1664) inherited the estate on the death of his father in 1629. A Terrier of the estates made in 1630 and 1631 shows that he was the lord of the manors of Boxted Hall in Suffolk; Horndon House, Ardenhall in Horndon-on-the-Hill, Essex; Barrowhall and Adams Fee in Great Wakering, Essex.

The Terrier also gives a description of the land around Boxted Hall '. . . the Manor or Mancion Howse called Boxsted Hall with the buildinges yardes & garden within the Moate, the Court yarde with the Bowling ground therein, lying right before the Howse, the Stable, the Dovehowse & Dovehowse garden, the high howse, thold orchyard (encompassing the moate round about the Mancion howse), the Newe orchyard & the Church hill lying up to the Church with the warren of Conyes . . .' (6).

William was knighted by Charles I in 1631 and although he lived through the Civil War, the Commonwealth and the Restoration, he seems to have left few details of any involvement in national or local events. In his will, made in 1658, he requested that he be buried in the 'New Chapel' (the Poley chapel) '. . . privately in the night without any superflous pompe . . .' (7). The parish register records in 1664 that '. . . Sir William Poley, of Boxtead in the County of Suffolk, Knight, dyed their May 17 about 8 o'clock in the morning, and was buried the 18th of the same in the night about 11 or 12 o'clock . . .' (8).

He was succeeded by his son Sir John Poley (1638-1705) who was M.P. for Sudbury in 1688. In 1674 Boxted Hall was assessed for the Hearth Tax, as having 22 hearths.

The last Poley at Boxted was John (1676-1757) who, in 1754, settled the estate of 725 acres on his second cousin George, son of Elizabeth Poley and Robert Weller of Tunbridge Wells. The Boxted Overseers Account Book (9) shows that George Weller was living at the Hall in 1755, when as owner he first paid the parish Poor Rate.

John Poley died in 1757 having requested to be buried '. . . in the Burial place peculiar to my family in Boxtead Church, near the wall on the right hand as you enter . . .'. He bequeathed £2 a year for '. . . the necessary repairs of the said Burial Place, and in cleaning the monuments therein, and the two woodden Monuments in the chancel . . .'. Thomas Bridge his servant, was to receive an annuity of £100 and all his '. . . wearing clothes, wearing linnen, including shoes, wiggs, Hatts Gloves and Stockings' (10). He also requested that George Weller should take the additional surname of Poley, which he seems to have done in 1773, and thus the Weller Poley line began.

A letter of 5 November 1757 from James Nelthorpe to George Weller mentions the death of John Poley, the bequest to Thomas Bridge and the intended improvements to the hall '. . . You did not mention what disorder carried of the old Gentleman perhaps a total decay. I am most surprised at so large an Annuity to his Servant, I should have thought less might have been a sufficient reward for his Services. I find also many legacies, however I am glad you have the whole Estate at last. I wish you a succession of many happy Year's to enjoy it after you have made it compleat & elegant in every part . . .' (11).

The hall had been altered by 1767 when William Crofts, a descendant of the Poleys of Badley, wrote to George Weller '. . . my worthy good friend Mr Elwes has told me (the hall) is so much improved by your elegant taste' (12). Early 19th century engravings show the alterations included a Georgian stucco facade, the insertion of sash windows, and the addition of two bay windows on the ground floor.

George Weller Poley died in 1778 and was succeeded by his son, the Rev. John Weller Poley (1755-99). He purchased the Manor of Hartest including Hartest Farm in 1782, and by his marriage to Jane Blatch Whaley of Colchester in 1783 acquired Cooks and Sorrels Farms. He was also Rector of Hartest and Boxted 1791-99.

His son George Weller Poley (1783-1849) inherited the estate in 1799. At the time of the tithe surveys in 1839-41 he owned 793 acres or 58% of the land of Boxted; 477 acres or 24% in Hartest; 246 acres or 21% in Stanstead; 91 acres or 9% in Somerton and 91 acres or 6% in Hawkedon, making a total of 1,694 acres.

John George Weller Poley (1812-69) succeeded to the estate in 1849, and by his marriage to Diana Halifax of Chadacre Hall, united the two largest land owning families in Hartest. He was Deputy Lieutenant of the county, a magistrate and High Sheriff in 1857.

He was followed by his son John George Weller Poley (1849-1936) a magistrate and High Sheriff in 1883. In 1873 he owned 2,312 acres of land, at the rentable value of £2,506 a year (13).

Rev. Edmund Farrer visited Boxted Hall in 1905, and noted '. . . the house was once all half timbered, with plaster between but, I was told that in 1767, when Georgian windows were inserted, it was entirely covered with plaster. This remained till the present alteration, which is but of recent date . . .' (14). The timbered and gabled appearance of the hall is early Edwardian, only the position of the windows remaining from the earlier refronting.

John George Weller Poley was followed by his nephew Captain Edward Hallifax Weller Poley M.V.O. (1879-1948) who served with the Grenadier Guards in the Boer and First World Wars. He was also a magistrate, and High Sheriff in 1946.

He was succeeded by his son, Major John Halifax Weller Poley M.C. (1919-1976) who served with the Royal Artillery in the Second World War and was wounded three times. He was a magistrate, and served as High Sheriff in 1965.

His widow Nancy Weller Poley, is now Lady of the Manor of Boxted Hall, Boxted Moorehouse, and Hartest Hall.

The continuing link between the Weller Poley family and Boxted is ensured by Nancy's children Richard (b. 1948) and Toby (b. 1950), and by Richard's son Guy (b. 1975).

Throughout their 600 years at Boxted the Poley and Weller Poley family have been involved in the service of their country, both at home and abroad. They have been military commanders from the 15th to the 20th century; Members of Parliament in the 17th century; magistrates in the 19th and 20th centuries and have served in county positions including that of High Sheriff in successive generations. They have been linked by marriage to many of the landed and titled Suffolk families including Clopton of Melford, Hervey of Ickworth, Jermyn of Rushbrooke, Heigham of Barrow, Crofts of Saxham, D'Ewes of Stowlangtoft, Felton of Playford, Waldgrave of Bures and Halifax of Shimpling.

ARMS OF J. G. WELLER POLEY, ESQ., OF BOXTED.

1, Quarterly. 1 and 4, Poley. 2 and 3, Weller.*
2, Poley.
3, Badwell.
4, Leyes.
5, Knighton.
6, Weyland.
7, Rockell.
8, Blyant.
9, Shaa.

Arms of John George Weller Poley (1812–69): from 'Visitiation of Suffolk' by Joseph Howard (1866).

Boxted Hall c.1818.

Boxted Hall c.1930.

Weller Poley of Boxted

Maud, daughter of John Gislingham. = Thomas Pooley, of Codreth, Hertfordshire, called Thomas Poley, of Walsingham, Lord of the Manor of Boxted. = Anne, daughter and heir of Thomas Badwell of Boxted, Suffolk, sister of John Badwell, Esq., and as heir to him, Lady of the Manor of Boxted.

- Anne, mar. to Nicholas Lovell, gent.
- Rose
- John Poley, Parson of Stoke.
- Richard Pooley, son and heir, of Stoke Ash, in Suffolk, married Margaret, dau. of Simon Blyant of Thornham, Esq.
- Thomas Poley, eldest son by his second wife, Lord of the Manor of Boxted, in right of his mother, died 1461. = Alice, daughter of Geffrey Rookehill of Wormingford, Essex.
- Anne
- Abelyn

John Poley, son and heir, of Wormingford, Essex, Esq, died 1487. = Agnes, da. of Sir Richard Whethill, of Calais.

- Barbara, mar. to Darell, of Kent.
- George, Parson of Attleborough, Norfolk.
- Anthony
- John of Bedenham, Bedford.
- Richard Poley, son and heir, of Boxted, born c. 1468 at Boxted, and buried there 19 Feb, 1546. Will dated 3 March, 1541. His brass is in Boxted church. = Anne, daughter of Sir William Clopton of Long Melford, and of Liston Hall, Essex. Will dated 14 May, 1549, died 1550.
- Jane, mar. to Baker.

Children of Richard Poley and Anne:

- Thomazin mar. to Thomas Cornwell, of Wilsey Hall, Little Wratting.
- John Poley, Gent, son and heir, of Boxted, born c.1500, buried at Boxted 20 Aug. 1580. Granted manor to son in 1561. Founded charity in 1572. = Margery, daughter of John Blyant of Ringshall, and heir to Richard Blyant, her brother. She died 1561, bur. at Boxted, 20 Aug., 1561.
- Elizabeth, bapt. at Boxted 1540.
- Barbara, died unmarried.
- Richard Poley, Gent, born c.1515. Will dated 2 Apr. 1559, buried at Boxted 25 Apr. 1560. = Julyane, daughter of Judge Morgan, died 1563.

Children of John Poley and Margery:

- Anne, mar. to William Worlich of Wickhambrook, bapt. at Boxted 1567.
- Elizabeth, mar. to William Harvey, of Ickworth c.1553. Died 1616.
- Cuthbert
- Richard
- Giles, Vicar of Yaxley. = Alice Tender-love.
- William Poley, Gent, son and heir, buried at Boxted 18 Dec. 1587. = Alice, daughter and heir of Edmund Shae of Horndon-on-the-Hill, Essex, buried at Boxted 7 March 1577.
- Thomas Poley, of Wormingay, Norfolk. = Ann, da. of John Smith.

Children of Thomas Poley and Ann:

- Absolon Poley
- Sir John Poley, of Wormingay in Norfolk, Knight, 2nd son, married Abigail Wix. She died 1652. He died 1638, aged 80, both buried at Boxted.
- William Poley

First generation (children of the line above):

- Sir John Poley, son and heir, born c.1557, Knight of Boxted, died in Flanders c.1590.
- George, Bapt. at Boxted, 30 Dec. 1563.
- Anne, marr. Sir John Higham of Barrow, died 11 May 1623.
- Mary married George Colt, of Colts Hall, High Sheriff, of Suffolk 1580.
- Jane, Bapt. at Boxted, 31 Jan. 1564, marr. William Crofts of Lt. Saxham 19 Dec. 1599.
- Martha, buried at Boxted, 25 March, 1580.
- Alice, married Waldegrave Abel, of Nether Hall, West Bergholt, Essex, married at Boxted, 5 Oct., 1585.
- Sir William Poley, Kt., of Boxted, bapt. there 23 Dec., 1562, married at Rushbrook, 20 Sep., 1597, M.P. for Sudbury, 1623 and 1628, died 5 August, burd. at Boxted, 6 Aug., 1629. = Anne, 2nd Dau. of Sir Robert Jermyn, Knight, of Rushbrooke, burd. at Boxted, 4th April, 1658.

Second generation (children of Sir William Poley and Anne):

- Judith Poley, bapt. at Rushbrooke 1st August, 1598, marr. at St. Mary, Bury, 3rd Feb., 1615, died 9 June, burd. at Boxted, 1661. = Sir Humphrey May, Kt., Chancellor of the Duchy of Lancaster, burd. at Boxted, 1661.
- Robert Poley, Esq., eldest son, killed at the Isle of Rhe.
- Elizabeth, daughter of Sir Henry Arden, Kt., of Warwickshire, 1st wife burd. at Boxted, 23 June, 1632. = Sir Wm. Poley, Kt., of Boxted, bapt. at Rushbrooke, 15th Aug., 1602, died 17th burd. 28th May, 1664, at Boxted. = Elizabeth, 5th dau. of Paul D'Ewes, of Stowlangtoft, 2nd wife, born 23 Jan. 1617, burd. at Boxted 5th April 1698.
- Sir John Poley, Kt., of Bury, bapt. at Rushbrooke, 6th Nov., 1603, marr. at Rougham on 21st April, 1653, died 9 Nov., 1664, burd. at Boxted. = Catherine, daughter of Dr. Jasper, Despontine of Bury St. Edmunds, buried 12th Aug., 1670, at Boxted.
- Katherine Poley, bapt. at Rushbrooke, 29th March, 1600, died 1665, burd. at Boxted=Edward Barker, son of Sir Robert Barker, burd. at Boxted.
- Mary Poley, bapt. at St. Mary, Bury, 17th Oct., 1616.

Third generation (children of Sir Wm. Poley and Elizabeth D'Ewes):

- Ann Poley
- 1, Elizabeth, only dau. of George Walden, of Lt. Bursted, Essex. 1st wife, burd. 28th Jan., 1677, at Boxted. =2, Bridget, dau. of Richard Samms, of Lt. Totham, and widow of Thomas Roberts of Braxtead, Essex, Esq., 2nd wife bur. at Boxted, 23rd Dec., 1689. = Sir John Poley, Kt. of Boxted, son and heir, baptised there 22 Jan., 1637, married 1664, M.P. for Sudbury 1688, died 13th, burd. at Boxted 15th Sept., 1705. =3, Dorothy, daughter of Sir Henry Felton of Playford, widow of Maurice Claxton of Livermere, 3rd wife died 1713.
- Thomas Poley, Esq., born 28 Aug., 1642 at Boxted, died 1701. = Frances, da. of Sir Richard Head, of Rochester.
- Elizabeth Poley born 2 Nov., 1639, at Boxted= William Clopton, of Liston, Esq.
- Cecilia Poley, born 4 July, 1645, at Boxted=Thomas Brown, Esq., of Arlsey, Bedfordshire, marr. at Boxted 1668.
- William Poley, born 13 Mar, 1647, drowned at Liston, 14 Feb., 1711, aged 64, burd. at Boxted.

Wm. Poley, born 17th Oct., 1674, burd. 28th Feb., 1675 at Boxted

John Poley, Esq., bapt. at Boxted, 29th July, 1676, burd. there 14th Sept., 1757. Last Poley of Boxted. Settled estate on George Weller in 1754.

Elizabeth Poley, bapt. at Boxted, 11th Jan., 1682, died unmarried 11th Oct., 1726.

William Poley, born 2nd Feb., 1684, at Boxted, burd. there 25 April, 1698.

Elizabeth Poley, eldest daughter, born 2nd Dec., 1681, died 13th May, 1761. = Robert Weller, Esq. of Tunbridge, Kent, born 12th March, 1676, died 18th Sept., 1751.

Richard Poley, born 8th Jan., 1682=Elizabeth Wilford, died 1770.

William Poley

Bridget Poley

George Weller Poley, Esq., only son and heir, born 30th May, 1710, died 29th Dec., 1778, burd. at Boxted. First Weller Poley. = Frances, dau. of Thomas Hussey, of Burwash, Sussex, Esq., died at Long Melford, 24th Oct., 1796, aged 73, burd. at Boxted.

Robert Weller Poley, borne 12th July, 1756, died 2 Aug., 1756.

George Weller Poley, eldest son, died unmarried, 10th April, 1780, aged 26, burd. at Boxted.

Rev. John Weller Poley, of Boxted Hall, born 23rd April, 1755, died 29th May, 1799, aged 44. = Jane, dau. of John Blatch Whaley, Esq., of Colchester, died 20 Dec., 1833, aged 74.

Frances Poley, died July, 1835. = Rev. Walter Maurice Johnson of Spalding, Lincolnshire, vicar of Weston, died 1832.

Edward W. Poley, born 30th May, 1758, died 17 Feb., 1764.

Francis W. Poley

Rev. William Weller Poley, of Hartest, born 12th August, 1765, died 15th Feb., 1837, aged 72.

George Weller Poley, Esq., only son, of Boxted Hall, born 1st Nov., 1783, married 8th March, 1808, died Nov. 5th, 1849, aged 66. = Helen Sophia, dau. of James Fisher, Esq., of Browston Hall, Suffolk.

Charlotte Helen Weller Poley, born 23 June, 1809 =1843 Peter Hamilton Capt. R.N.

Marianne Jane Weller Poley, born 2 July, 1810.

John George Weller Poley, born 16 Jan, 1812, married 28 Oct., 1847, at Shimpling, died 5th Sept., 1869. = Diana, da. of Thos. Halifax, Esq., of Chadacre Hall, Suffolk, died 1884.

Jane Mary Weller Poley, born 13 March, 1813=19 April, 1836, Michael Cullen Cotton, Esq., of Dover.

Rev. William Weller Poley, born 18 Nov. 1814, marrd. 13 Oct., 1846. Rector of Santon Downham, died 1887. = Margaret, only child of Rev. J. Tyers Barrett, Rector of Attleborough, Norfolk.

Helen Sophia Weller Poley, born 23 April, 1816.

Georgiana Frances Weller Poley, born 8 Sept., 1817, died Dec., 1817.

Charles Edward Weller Poley, born 15 March, 1819, died 1890.

James Fisher Weller Poley, born 15 June, 1821, died 21 April, 1842.

George Frederic Weller Poley, born 1823, died 1864.

Walter Johnson Weller Poley, born 1826.

Frances Weller Poley= Sir Richard Gethia.

John George Weller Poley, born 25 May, 1849, marrd. 19 June, 1900, died 4 June, 1936. = Ethel dau. of Rev. Stenning Johnson of Itchenor, Sussex, Died 6 Sept, 1936.

Thomas Weller Poley, born 8 Nov., 1850, marrd. 8 Aug., 1879, died 29 Dec., 1924. = Eleanor dau. of John Jonston, Q.C. of West Broyle, Sussex, died 1944.

Edward Hallifax Weller Poley, born 6 July, 1879, marrd. 21 March, 1916, died 12 June, 1948. = Ursula, dau. of Rear-Adm. John Hallifax, she died 24 July, 1977.

Sheila Mary Weller Poley, born 2 Oct., 1917, marr. 1st 11 May, 1940, 2nd 12 July, 1966. = 1, Sir Otho Prior Palmer 2. Louis Cyril de Chazel

John Hallifax Weller Poley, born 22 April, 1919, marrd. 3 Feb., 1947, died Dec. 1976. = Nancy, dau. of Maj. Ivor Buxton of Shelly Hall, widow of Lt-Col. John Loveday.

Hugh Thomas Weller Poley, born 7 Aug., 1922, killed on active service 15 Sept., 1942.

Nicholas Toby Weller Poley, born 6 Jan., 1950

Richard Hallifax Weller Poley, born 11 Aug. 1948, marrd. 24 Sept., 1970. = Sarah Francesa, dau. of John Gosling of Woolards Ash, Essex, born 2 June, 1951.

Annabelle Rose Weller Poley, born 25th Feb., 1980.

Guy Hallifax Weller Poley, born 22 Jan., 1975.

Katherine Francesca Weller Poley, born 17 Jan., 1973.

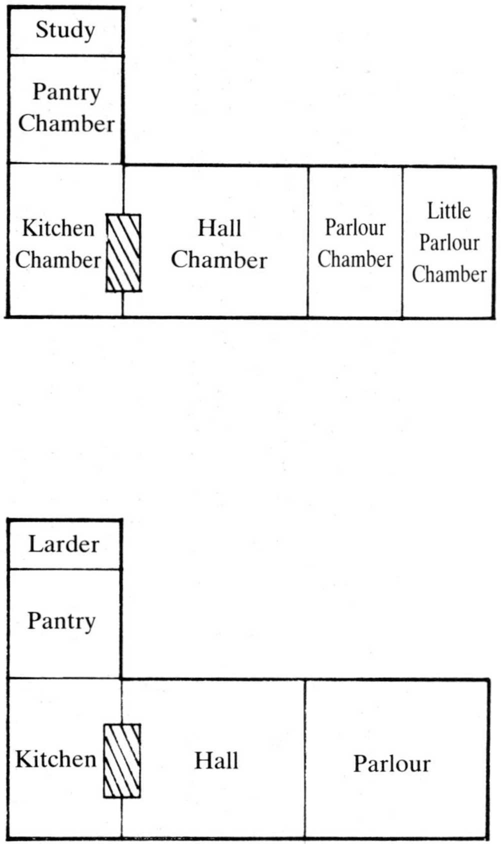

Possible ground floor plan of 'Kings in 1616.

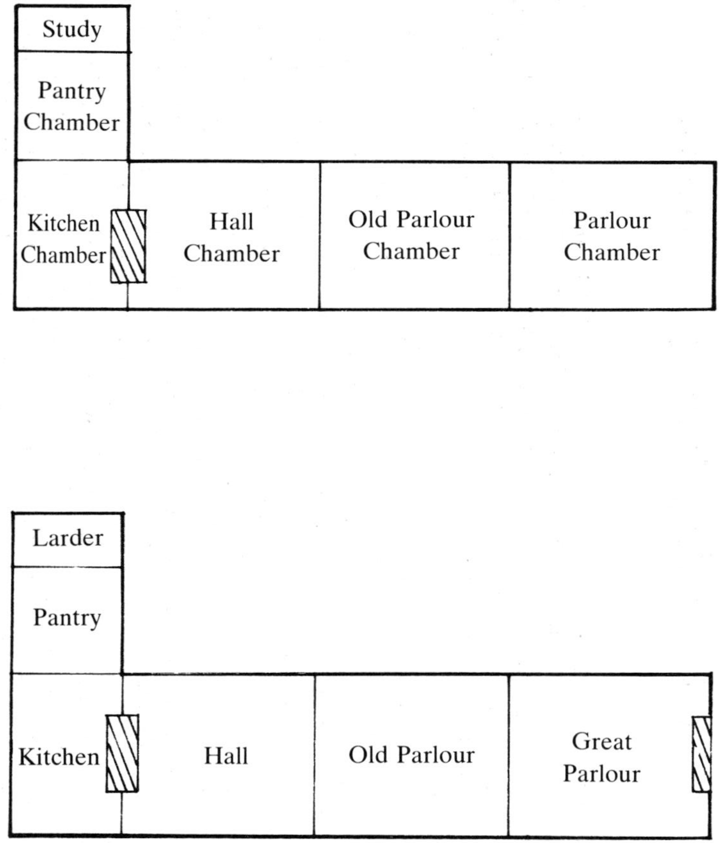

Possible ground floor plan of 'Kings' in 1665.

The Cronshay Family of 'Kings'

The Cronshay family came to Hartest in 1580 and continued in the neighbourhood until the late 18th century. This section traces their link with an as yet unidentified house called 'Kings'. The details of the family have been taken from the parish register and their wills. The probate inventories have enabled us to show the changes in the use and status of the various rooms of the house.

Thomas Cronshay who had been Rector of Hartest and Boxted since 1580, was buried at Hartest in December 1615. His will (1) made a year earlier reveals details about both his family and the houses and lands that he owned.

He lived in a house called 'Kings', which he had enfranchised or changed from a copyhold to a freehold property. His son John (1587-1619) Rector of Fakenham and Euston, was to inherit 'Kings' and another enfranchised house called 'Appletons' (now Pickles Farm) with 31 acres of land. Another son Thomas (b.1589) Rector of Chilton was bequeathed £100; Richard (b.1590) a house and 38 acres ; Robert (1592-1664) a house and 33 acres; Joseph (1594-1651) £100; Mary (b.1585) a debt of £60 which William Stansby her husband owed; Francis (b.1586) wife of Thomas Negus £100.

An inventory (2) of all his goods was made by five Hartest men in January 1616. 'Kings' was a large property and probably 'L' shaped in plan. A suggested reconstruction of the plan is shown opposite. On the ground floor were the Kitchen, Hall, Parlour in one wing, and the Pantry and Larder with the cellar below in the other wing. The first floor rooms were a Parlour Chamber and Little Parlour Chamber, over the Parlour, a Hall Chamber over the Hall, Kitchen and Pantry Chambers, and probably the Study over the Larder. The second floor contained just an upper chamber which was most likely over the Parlour Chambers (3). Other buildings listed in the inventory were the Dairy House, Brewing House, Backhouse, Stable, Workhouse, Mill House and Barn.

The room used for the preparation and cooking of food was the Kitchen which contained: a Jack with weights (a mechanical device for turning the spit), three spits, a pair of cobirons (supports for a spit), an iron dripping pan, frying pans, two gridirons, two tramells (large pot hooks), three bass potts, a 'brazing posnit' (a three legged cooking pot for placing in the fire), six kettles (open cooking pots), two basting spoons, two chafing dishes (a heated dish for keeping food warm), a dresser, chopping blocks, two cleavers, a shrelling knife, two old stools, a pair of bellows, three pails, a pair of shears and a pair of candle snuffers.

The adjoining Pantry had a table, all the pewter items, a flasket (shallow washing tub), trenchers (wooden plates), potts and bottles. The Larder House contained a trough, a powdering tub (for salting meat), a pair of mustard querns (for grinding the seeds), another chopping block and pair of shears. In the Celler were four hogsheads (large casks) and other vessels.

The Cronshay Family of 'Kings'

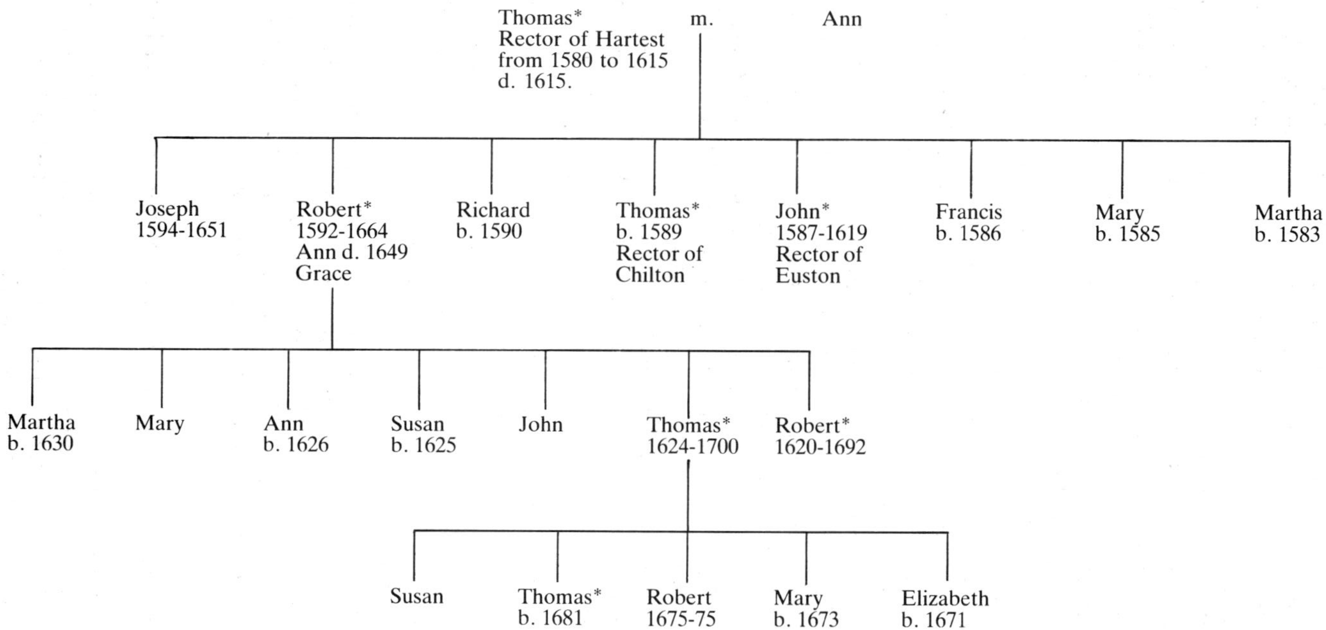

* against a name indicates an owner of 'Kings'.

The Hall, which was the only other heated room in the house, contained three tables, two forms (benches), three chairs, two stools, in the fireplace were a pair of cobirons and a frying pan, and a 'stained cloth' (decorated or painted) hung on one wall.

Around the walls of the Parlour was wainscot, or wooden panelling, which Thomas specified had to be retained along with the glass in the windows. The furniture in the room comprised a table, a form, a cupboard, a press (wardrobe), a posted bed (with a canopy, or tester, on four posts), and a trundle bed (a low bed which could be stored below one of ordinary height during the day, used by children or servants).

Upstairs the Kitchen Chamber had a posted bed, a trundle bed, a table and a hutch (small chest, often for storing clothes). Also stored in the room were a 'Coslett furnished' (a piece of body armour) and part of a musket. The Pantry Chamber contained a table, a small hutch, a half-headed bed (one with a headboard only) and a trundle bed. The Study had a chair and table and 'the shelves with the books'.

The Hall Chamber contained a canopy bed, a trundle bed, a table, a form, a livery table (table for standing a small livery cupboard on), a chair, a stool and a carpet. The linen was also stored in the room and included fifteen pairs of sheets, thirty-six napkins, nine table cloths, two pillowbears (pillow cases) and twelve towels. The Little Parlour Chamber, which also seems to have been over the downstairs Parlour, had a posted bed, a trundle bed, a pallet bed (just a mattress), a table and two forms.

The Upper Chamber, which was probably an attic over the Parlour Chamber and reached by a ladder, contained a store of cheese, butter, wheat and fruit.

The Dairy and Brewing House contained cheese and butter making equipment and brewing vessels. The workhouse and barn contained agricultural tools and equipment including saws, hatchets, spades, shovels, wedges, screen, a cart,a tumbrell, a pair of harrows, a plough, two ladders and a pair of wheels. In the barn were also wheat, barley, bullimong and hay. The livestock comprised seven horses, two colts, twenty-five sheep, nine milk cows, two bullocks, a bull, two calves, four shotts, a pig and the poultry. The mill house contained a horse-mill.

The total valuation of Thomas Cronshay's possessions not including the houses and lands, came to £576 11s. 8d. which can be broken down as follows: 'ready money' £232 5s. 6d. or 40.3%; agricultural goods £130 3s. or 22.6%. debts owing to him £109 7s. 4d. or 19%; and household goods £104 15s. 10d. or 18.1% of the total valuation.

The Second Generation: John, Thomas and Robert Cronshay

John Cronshay, Rector of Euston, inherited 'Kings' in 1616 and died in 1619, having bequeathed it to his brother Thomas the Rector of Chilton. He in turn sold it to another brother Robert who died in 1664, and whose will (4) and inventory (5) have both survived.

Robert (1592-1664) described himself as a gentleman, was married twice and had five children still living when he made his will in 1664. These were Robert (1620-1692) who inherited 'Kings' in the third generation; Thomas (b.1624) who was bequeathed a house at Millend; John who had the Kiln House; Ann (b.1626) and Mary.

The inventory, made on the death of Robert in 1664, shows that an additional heated room, called the 'Great Parlour' with a chamber above it, had been constructed next to the earlier Parlour, which now became known as the 'Old Parlour'.

The kitchen was again the main room for preparing and cooking food. The items of furniture recorded were a table, a form, two dressers, four chairs and three stools. The kitchen utensils present were two dripping pans, a Jack, five spits, three tramells and the iron bar on which they hung, a pair of tongs, a fire pan, two gridirons, three pairs of pothooks, a pair of bellows, three smoothing irons, two pails, and a pair of andirons.

Brass and pewter items were listed separately, and may have been on shelves or in a chest, these were seven brass kettles, seven candlesticks, two posnets, a colander, a skimmer (for skimming cream), four pots, two spoons, two pans, a chafer (small closed brazier containing hot ash or charcoal, for heating a chafing dish), four chafing dishes, and thirty-eight pieces of pewter.

The Pantry had five shelves, a dresser, an empty firkin, a firkin of butter, three sacks of meal, a linen press, a linen basket, a maund (a hand basket), a pair of brass scales, a peel (long handled implement for removing bread from an oven), a fly keep (presumably to keep them off!). In the larder were eight shelves, two chopping blocks, a mortar and pestle, a pair of musten querns, three leather bottles, twenty four trenchers and six wooden dishes. The cellar contained four hogsheads, two barrels and three alestools (stands for barrels).

The Hall was the first of the living rooms to be described, and contained two tables, two forms, two chairs, six cushions, a glass case, two pair of andirons in the fireplace, and a pair of beam scales with thirteen lead weights. Also present was a collection of weapons comprising four swords, a musket, a pair of bandoliers (belts for carrying musket and shot), a halberd (a combined spear and axe), and a headpiece (helmet).

The original parlour was now known as the 'Old Parlour' and contained a posted bed with a feather mattress, two bolsters, two blankets, a pillow, a coverlett, curtains and curtain rods, a half headed bed with a feather mattress, two feather bolsters, a feather pillow, three blankets and a coverlett, a second half headed bed with a flock mattress; a cupboard, four chests and curtains (presumably at the windows). In the will the posted bed was described as being the one on which his son Robert lay.

The new 'Great Parlour' had many fine furnishings, a long table, a carpet for the table, five joined stools, a livery cupboard with a carpet (a small ventilated cupboard for food and drink), seven joined chairs, six of which were 'wrought' (turned), four joined stools 'all wrought' , a looking glass, a pair of andirons in the fireplace, a pistol, a map and 'certayne pictures'.

Upstairs a fireplace had been inserted into the kitchen chamber since 1616 and contained, a pair of andirons, a pair of tongs and a firepan. The rest of the furniture in the room was a posted bed, a trundle bed, four trunks, four chests one of which contained pewter, a table, a wicker chair, two chairs, two cushions, a small table and a three shelves.

In the Pantry Chamber were a Canopy bed, trundle bed, a trunk, three chairs and six stools.

The Hall Chamber contained a posted bed (blankets etc. are listed in the inventory), a trundle bed, two tables, two chests, four stools, two bilstaves (halberds) and an old musket. A trunk in the room contained linen, which was detailed in his will as being twelve pair of sheets, six broad cloths, eighteen napkins, a burying cloth and a Christening kerchief.

The Old Parlour Chamber was used for the storage of wheat, halters, eight fleeces, two bushels, a peck, half peck and eight sacks. In contrast to the Old Parlour, the new one contained a posted bed, a trundle bed, a settle (bench with back and arms), a long table with a carpet, two joined stools, a chest, a livery cupboard with a carpet, four joined and covered chairs, three joined and covered stools, five cushions, two pairs of curtains with a valance, two carpets and two curtains 'hanging before the windows'.

The vaulted floor (the 'Upper Chamber' of 1616) was still used for storage, and had bullimong, a screen, a still (stand for a barrel), a jack and 'some lumber'.

The outhouses contained the various cheese and butter making equipment, brewing vessels and a horse mill as before. The agricultural equipment included working tools such as various saws, swath rakes, hatchets, forks, spades, shovels, flails, fans; a cart, a pair of wheels, two tumbrels, a pair of harrows, a roller and a plough. The livestock included, three mares, a colt, seven cows, a bullock, two shoats (half grown pigs) and sheep.

At the end of the inventory were summary valuations of books including a Bible and Foxes Book of Martyrs, and of 'plate' in the house. Details from the will show the 'plate' to have included two silver spoons and a gilt cup.

The total valuation of 'Kings' in 1664 was £363 11s. 8d., of which £140 13s. 8d. or 38.7% was in household goods, £113 or 31.1% in debts or plate, and £109 18s. or 30.2% in agricultural equipment, livestock and produce.

The Third Generation: Robert and Thomas Cronshay

Robert Cronshay (1620-1692) inherited 'Kings' from his father in 1664. He was a bachelor, died intestate and administration of the estate was granted to Thomas his brother. Robert was buried on 9 September, aged 72 and an inventory of the movable goods taken 26 September 1692.

The inventory (6) only lists the Kitchen, Hall, Old Parlour and Parlour on the ground floor, and the Parlour Chamber and Closet on the first floor. All the rooms are very sparsely furnished the total valuation only amounted to £15 6s.

It may be that Robert had already assigned most of his goods to his brother, and therefore they were not assessed by the valuers. If Thomas was sharing the house it meant that he had all the first floor rooms, except the Parlour Chamber, including the heated Kitchen Chamber. In the 1674 Hearth Tax it was Thomas and not Robert who was assessed for four fireplaces.

Thomas (1624-1700) seems to have certainly had the property after the death of Robert. On his own death in June 1700 aged 76, his estate included the whole of 'Kings'. The inventory (7) shows that the house had the same number of rooms as in the 1664 list, the only improvement being a fireplace inserted into the newer Parlour Chamber.

The Kitchen contained the usual assortment of cooking utensils including twenty-two pewter dishes, two plates, three porringers (porridge pot), a salt cellar, two old flagons, two pewter candlesticks, five brass candlesticks, two basins, a chamber pot, a warming pan, four kettles, an iron pot, a brass pot, six skillets, two jacks, five spits, three gridirons, three pails, a pair of cobirons in the hearth, three tramells, a pair of tongs and a pair of bellows. The furniture consisted of a small table, two stools, four chairs and a form.

The Pantry contained a pair of mustard querns, two pestle and mortars, a dripping pan and a stool. In the larder were dishes, spoons, trenchers and earthenware vessels.

The living rooms on the ground floor were more sparsely furnished than in 1664. The Hall contained three forms, three chairs, three glass keeps, earthenware, a fire pan, a pair of tongs and a pair of cobirons, a rolling pin and a batteldor (wooden implement, shaped like a cricket bat, for smoothing linen after washing).

The former 'Old Parlour' was now called the 'Little Parlour'. The beds present in 1664 had been removed, and only two presses and two hutches remained. The 'Great Parlour' of 1664 was not mentioned in this inventory. Perhaps all former fine furnishings had been removed and the room stood empty.

Upstairs the Kitchen Chamber had a feather bed, a rug, two chests, a chest with drawers, a livery cupboard, three stools, a small table, four window curtains and rods, a looking glass, and a pair of cobirons in the fireplace. The Pantry Chamber contained only a half-headed bed and two old stools. The 'Closet' which was probably the 'Study' of 1616 contained 'a parcell of bookes'.

The Hall Chamber contained a feather bed and a trundle flock bed, a small table, two hutches, a trunk, a chest, two boxes, three stools, a chair and a form.

The Little Parlour Chamber had two old beds, two forms, a powdering tub and a glass keep. The now heated Parlour Chamber over the 'Great Parlour' retained something of its former comfort, having a bed, two chests, a chest of drawers, a livery cupboard, a box, a small table, four stools, four window curtains and rods, a looking glass, and a pair of cobirons in the fireplace.

The 'vaulted floor' of 1664 was now called the 'Garrett' and was used for the storage of unwanted household items. These included 'a parcell of old

Armor' which must have been the collection displayed in the Hall in 1664. Other items stored there were seven old broken chairs, four old stools, a table, two trunks and a basket.

Outside the Dairy and Brewhouse contained the usual assortment of equipment and vessels. The livestock consisted of six cows, two calves, a horse, a mare, two hogs and 'sheep'. The crops still growing were wheat, barley, bullimong and grass. There were also several handtools, a pair of harrows, two ploughs and a horse mill.

The total valuation came to £110 7s. of which £84 9s. 6d. or 73.7% was in agricultural equipment, livestock and produce, and only £15 17s. 6d. or 26.3% in household goods.

The link between the Cronshay family and 'Kings' was broken in 1711 when Thomas, a yeoman, the heir of Thomas, sold it to Thomas Sargent (8).

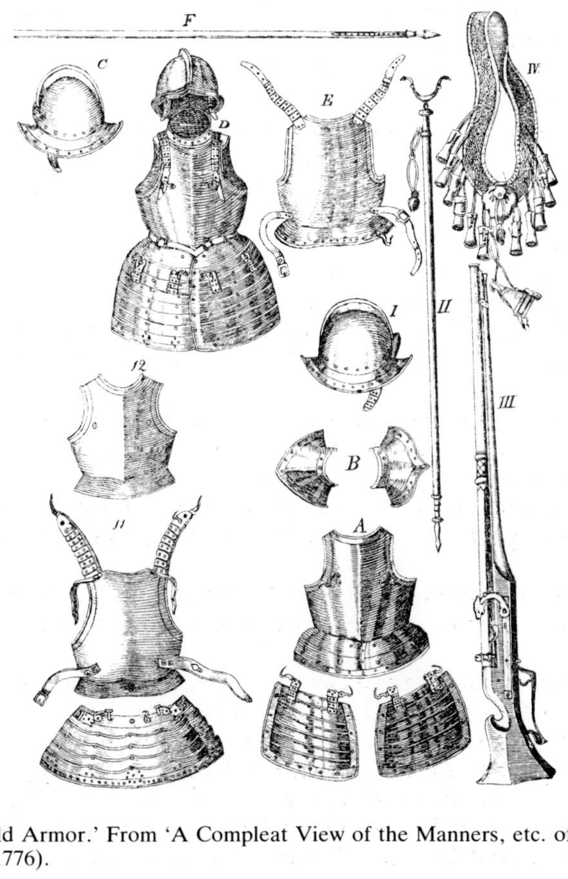

'a parcell of old Armor.' From 'A Compleat View of the Manners, etc. of England' by Joseph Srutt Vol. 3 (1776).

The Underwoods of Hartest

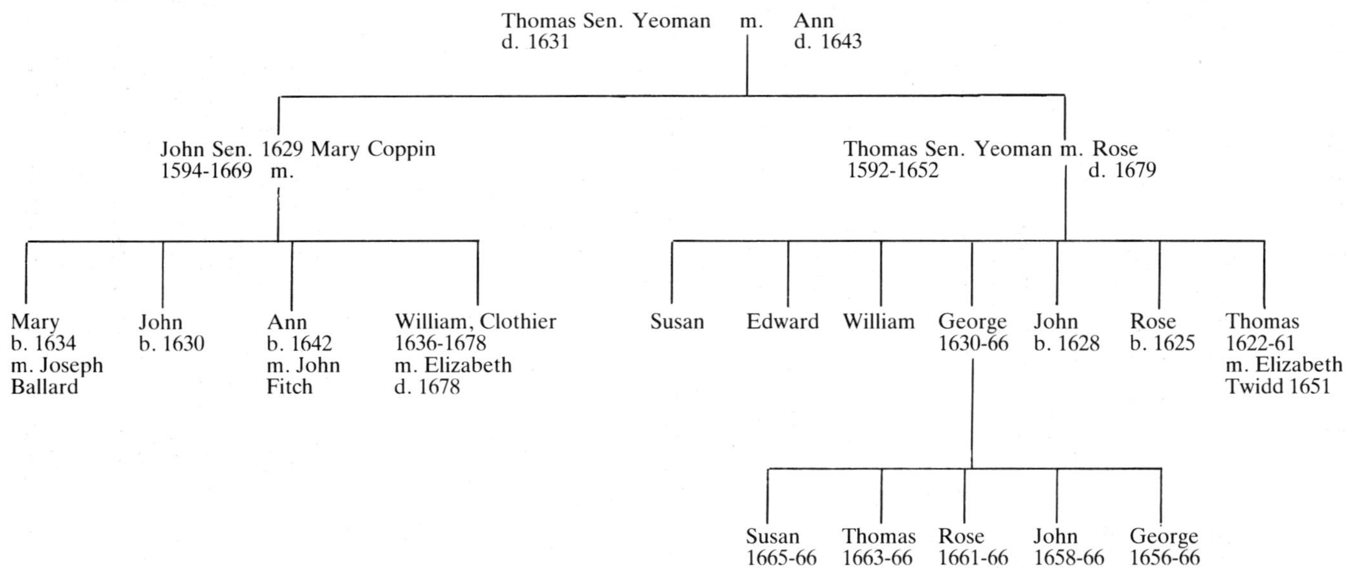

The Underwood Family

Thomas Underwood senior, yeoman died in 1631. He lived at a house still called 'The Hatch' (1). Evidence from the parish register shows he was married to Ann, who survived him until 1643, and had two sons Thomas (b.1592) and John (b.1594). He bequeathed £1 to the poor of Hartest; £1 to his son Thomas; £1 to his grandson Thomas; and the residue of the estate to his second son John, on condition £5 was paid to his wife Ann every year. He was illiterate and made his mark at the concusion of his will.

Thomas (1592-1652), a yeoman, and son of Thomas was married to Rose, who died in 1679. They had seven children who survived into adulthood, Thomas (b.1622) mentioned in his grandfather's will, Rose (b.1625), John (b.1628), George (b.1630), William, Edward and Susan. He appears to have owned two properties one where he dwelt, and another called 'Sorrells' (2). The exact site of the latter is uncertain, but was situated on the east side of the road between Cooks and Kew Garden Farm. In 1788 the site was described as '. . . the ground whereon a Messuage or Tenement called Sorrells lately stood and since pulled down . . .' (3). The house and land amounted to eighteen acres and was owned, along with Cooks Farm, by Ralph Twidd who leased it to Thomas Underwood (4).

The contents of the two properties, and the crops and livestock belonging to them were itemised in the probate inventory taken after his death in February 1652 (5). Sorrells had a Hall, Dairy and Brewhouse on the ground floor; a Hall Chamber and 'Chambers' on the first floor; and two barns outside. There was very little furniture in the house, the hall contained two tables, a keep (cupboard) a form, two chairs, a pair of cobirons, a firepan, a pair of tongs, a pair of tramells. The Hall chamber contained only two beds; the Dairy had cheese making utensils and the Brewhouse only bricks. Wheat and barley was stored in the Chambers on the first floor of the house. The Barn contained the hay, corn, wheat, barley, a screen, a swath rake, cows, bullocks and horses; a second barn contained more corn and hay and also some cheese.

The unnamed house where he lived, had a Hall, Parlour Chamber, Kitchen Chamber and Buttery Chamber on the first floor.

The Hall contained two tables, two forms, a cupboard, four chairs, a glass keep and 144 trenchers (wooden plates). The Parlour had twelve jointed stools, a table, three chairs, a livery cupboard, a table chair (a chair with a hinged back, which is brought forward to rest on the arms to form the table), six cushions, a pair of cobirons, a firepan and tongs. From this latter group of items it is obvious that the Parlour had a fireplace.

On the other side of the chimney stack was the kitchen, with four spits, cobirons, two fire pans, two pairs of tongs, two tramells, a keep, a small table and a form. Also present in the room were a musket, a fowling piece, four flitches of bacon and an unspecified number of brass and pewter items.

The Buttery contained three hogsheads, three barrels, three bottles, and a pair of querns for grinding mustard seed. In the Dairy were a cheese press, two powdering tubs and a powdering trough (for salting meat) four cheese mots, two cheesebreads, scales and weights. The Backhouse had brewing vessels, a pair of querns, a kneading trough (for bread) a meal hutch, and two combs of malt.

On the first floor the Hall Chamber contained a bed and a hanging press (wardrobe) which were described in his will as a 'posted bed and a great press'. Also in the room were a wicker chair, two small jointed stools, a small table and four books. The Parlour Chamber had a bed, four chairs, two stools and a livery table. The Kitchen and Buttery Chambers each contained only two beds and a chest.

Outside were a cart, two tumbrels, ploughs, harrows, two hoggs, poultry and four acres of wheat 'on the ground'.

The total valuation of his moveable goods was £373 15s. 8d. of which 25.4% was in household items and 74.6% in livestock, crops and implements. The agricultural total can be divided into crops 45.4%, cows 28%, other livestock 12.5%, cheese 10.7% and implements 3.3%.

John Underwood (1594-1669) was the second son of Thomas who died in 1631 and brother of Thomas who died in 1652. He described himself as a yeoman, married Mary Coppin in 1629 and had four children who survived into adulthood, John (b.1630) Mary (b.1634). William (b.1636) and Ann (b.1642). He owned several properties '. . . the tenement wherein I now dwell' (which can be identified as 'Cranmer'); two houses or cottages '. . . at or neere unto the green called Cross greene . . .' then occupied by Christopher Wallis and Thomas Reed, and possibly the 'Hatch' occupied by his son John (6).

His wife Mary was to have 'Cranmer' for life and then it was to pass to his youngest son William, together with half its contents on condition he paid £30 to his sister Ann. She was married to John Fitch and they had a son also called John. Ann was to inherit the two cottages at Cross Green and half the contents of 'Cranmer' on the death of her mother. Mary married Joseph Ballard in 1657, they had a son named Joseph, and she was only to inherit 5s. John who lived at the 'Hatch' was also to receive only 5s.

The probate inventory (7) taken in 1669, itemised the contents of the house called 'Cranmer' where John lived. It consisted of a Hall, Parlour, Low Chamber, Buttery Dairy, Cheese Chamber and various outhouses.

The Hall contained a long table, two forms, two glass keeps, a small table, four chairs, four stools, two tramells, a spit, a pair of andirons, a pair of tongs, a gridiron and a sack. In the Parlour were a bed, a trundle bed, two hutches, three chairs, three stools, three cushions, a hanging press and a warming pan.

The Low Chamber had a feather bed, a cupboard and a livery cupboard. In the Buttery were brass and pewter items, three beer vessels and four tubs. The Dairy contained a cheesepress, a cheese tub, a powdering tub, two kellers, two pails, four cheese mots and a kneading trough. In the Cheese chamber were the cheeses and two riddles. The household linen was listed in detail as six pair of sheets, two board cloths (table cloths), eighteen napkins and six pillow beers (pillow cases).

Outside were 2 cows, a hog, an old cart, an old tumbrel, a mashing tub and a long ladder.

The total valuation amounted to £55 18s. of which household items, including brewing equipment, clothes and debts represented 56%; and the hay, corn, cart, tumbrel, implements, two cows and a hog represented 44% of the total.

The third generation of the Underwood family in the 17th century were the children of Thomas and John. Thomas, son of Thomas and grandson of Thomas, was born in 1622, married Elizabeth Twidd (perhaps the daughter of his landlord Ralph Twidd) in 1651, and died aged 39 in 1661. His probate inventory shows him to have been involved in the cloth trade, supplying merchants at Cavendish and Norwich. This aspect is more fully discussed in the Cloth Trade section.

The family of his brother George suffered in the great plague when George himself aged 36, and five of his children aged between seventeen months and ten years all died in October 1666.

The only documentary evidence to survive about the children of John Underwood, refers to his youngest son William. He was to inherit 'Cranmer' on the death of his mother, who outlived him and died in 1696. William (1636-78) a Clothier, made his will on 1 August 1678 and was buried on the 5th. He made several alternative provisions in his will because his wife Elizabeth was '. . . now big with child and I know not how it may please God to deale with her' (8). Elizabeth made her will on 26 August 1678 and was buried on 15 September, she included clauses in her will to take effect if the child 'I am now bigge withall shall chance to live . . . or . . . happen to dye . . .' (9). The baptism of the child is not recorded in the parish register and it seems most likely that it died with Elizabeth.

William was living at Cranmer at the time of his death and the probate inventory (10) shows there were more first floor rooms than recorded in 1669. The house comprised of a Hall, Parlour, a little room, Buttery, Dairy and a Tubhouse on the ground floor, with a Hall Chamber, Buttery Chamber, and Cheese Chamber on the first floor. Most of the furniture valued in 1669 was still there in 1678. The Hall contained a long table, two forms, five chairs, a little table, a glass case, two Bibles and other books, a jack, three spits, four pairs of cobirons, three tramells, three fire pans, two pair of tongs, two gridirons and two smoothing irons.

In the Parlour were a bed, a table, nine buffet stools, three chairs, a table chair, a livery cupboard, a chest, six cushions, a chest, a small trunk, three boxes, two dressing baskets and a warming pan. The little room contained a press cupboard, a little table, a chest, a glass case, three chairs, a little trunk, a buffet stool. The Butteries contained six barrels, two kneading troughs, a keep, a brass copper, five kettles (open cooking pots), two brass pots, an iron pot, three skillets (pot with short legs for placing near the fire), two frying pans and a powdering tub. The Dairy had a cheese press, a milk tray, a stone cooler and a cheese tub.

On the first floor the Hall Chamber had a high bed, a trundle bed, a wicker chair, a form and a buffet stool. The Buttery Chamber contained a bed, a hutch, a little table, a screen, two pair of scales and four lead weights. The Cheese Chamber housed cheese, butter, wheat and bullimong.

The crops and livestock outside consisted of corn, hay, four cows, a mare, a colt, two shoats and a cart. The largest valuation was for wool, yarn, tops and pack cloths which came to 45% of the total of £416 10s. 6d.

Sheep and Cattle: from 'A Book of Diverse devices' by Thomas Fella of Dunwich (1585–1622).

The Manor of Hartest Hall

Until 1561 the Manor of Hartest belonged to the Bishop of Ely, when it was 'exchanged' by the Crown under the terms of an Act of Parliament passed in 1559. Hartest Manor then became a part of the Royal Manor of East Greenwich.

One of the ways that the Crown could increase the income from its manors was to sell, or enfranchise, copyhold property. Some time between 1580-1614 the Rector of Hartest purchased his house called 'Kings', and another house called 'Appletons' with 31 acres of land from the Crown (1).

In 1608 the copyholders of Hartest petitioned the Earl of Salisbury, Lord High Treasurer, complaining of their poverty and asking that both the annual rents and the fines should be fixed at the same rates as had been levied 'time out of memory' (2). The petition stated that Hartest is a 'very small manor' with an income of only about £25 each year. The size of individual landholdings ranged from one to forty acres. Only two copyholders held 40 acres, three or four held 30 acres, 'others' had 20 acre holdings, 'some' held four, six, seven or ten acres each. Below these were forty cottagers described as 'small and poor copyholders' who had only two acres or less, and also thirty five householders who had 'no habitation or their own, nor cow nor calf'. The freeholders of the manor had left Hartest and let their lands at high rents to poor farmers.

In 1609 the Manor purchased from the Crown by George and John Salter. They must have sold it before 1644, when the earliest Court book surviving in 1765, shows Thomas Pooley to have been Lord of the Manor until at least 1652.

Thomas Turner of Oxford had purchased Hartest Manor before 1659 when the Court Roll for that year shows him to have been the Lord.

The Manor then passed through several members of the Turner family. Thomas was succeeded as Lord by his son Thomas from 1706-1729; he in turn by his brother George from 1729-34 and George's widow Penelope from 1733-1772. John Turner, a nephew then became Lord and in the same year was declared an insolvent debtor. The Manor of Hartest was mortgaged in order to pay his debts.

In April 1782 Rev. John Weller Poley of Boxted Hall, purchased the manor for £3,200, of which £2,923 was owed by Turner to his mortgagees. The amount of copyhold land belonging to the Manor was not specified. Only Hartest Farm (Lords Farm) was itemised, it contained 111 acres and was rented for £60 a year by Mr Cooper.

From 1782 the Manor devolved through successive members of the family, details of whom can be found under the section dealing with the Weller Poleys.

The Crown Inn, formerly Hartest Hall, c.1905: George Baynton then was both owner and occupier of the property.

Customs of the Manor

The earliest surviving list of manorial customs (3) for Hartest date from 1648 and was entered into a now missing Court Book 'A' covering the period 1644-1656. In 1765 the book was examined and the customs copied out as follows:–

1. That the custom of the Manor is from the Grandfather to the Youngest Son and from the Father to the Youngest Son, from the Youngest Son to the Eldest Son according to the Common Law, and from the Second Brother to the Eldest and not to the younger according to the Common Law. (This is the custom of property inheritance known as Borough English).
2. That the Custom is to fell and sell Timber Trees off the Copyholds without Licence of the Lord by a special Custom.
3. That by special Custom the Copholders may lett or demise their Copyhold Lands and Tenements from 3 years to 3 years, without Licence of the Lord of this Manor.
4. (Added by 1656) That the Tenants by special Custom may pull down any out House, without Licence of the Lord of the said Manor.

Hartest Hall alias The Crown Inn

Before the 1560s when the Manor of Hartest belonged to the Bishop of Ely, the Hall was probably the residence of the resident Steward. The impressive building on the northside, with its jettied upper story, was originally free-standing and may have been where the Manorial Courts were held.

Local tradition suggests that a part of the building now demolished on the east side, was the Guildhall of St Margaret of Antioch. However, it is more likely that the Guildhall stood on the site of the present 'Church Cottages' which was known as the 'Almshouse' at least since 1638 (4). The conversion to parish use as an almshouse or workhouse was the fate of many Guildhalls after the Reformation.

The earliest reference to Hartest Hall found so far, is in the will of John Bridge, yeoman in 1597 when he leaves his son William 'one Capital messuage in Hartest aforesaid called Hartest Hall helde by coppie of Court Roll of the Manor of Hartest aforesaid with three acers . . .' (5). That description of a building with three acres of ground continued to be used until the mid 19th century.

There is no firm evidence to indicate when the use of the building changed from a residence to an Inn. Francis Borley, who died in 1707 described the building as the 'Mansion house called Hartest Hall' as it continued to be known until some time before 1778. In that year Ann Butts, wife of the Bishop of Ely, who was the copyhold tenant, bequeathed to her daughter the Messuage 'called or known by the Name of the Crown Inn'. In 1805 Lydia Robinson surrendered the property to Stephen Baynton and described it as the '. . . Scite of the Manor of Hartest Hall, now called by the Name or Sign of The Crown Inn with 3 acres of meadow . . .' (6).

In August 1831 the antiquarian David Davy stayed at the Inn and made the following entry in his Journal '. . . Tuesday August 16, Returning to Shimpling, we set off for Hartest, where we hoped to find a public house, for sleeping: distance about 2 miles: after riding for near that space, we all at once came to the top of a steep hill, very steep for so flat a county as Suffolk; at the bottom of which appeared the village of Hartest; upon descending the hill, we came to the Public house we were in search of, & to our agreeable surprize, found an Inn, the Crown, where we met with most comfortable accommodations. We found our quarters here so agreeable, that we determined to make them our resting place for 2 or 3 nights, as long indeed as we could find work enough in the neighbourhood to employ us (7).

The Maxim family were landlords of the Crown from at least 1841 until about 1874. In the 1841 Census William Maxim, aged 40, was the publican at the Crown and his brother Joseph at the Bell. In 1851 William was also described as a farmer of 36 acres. His son Willoughby aged 25, had taken over by 1861 when he was described as a victualler, employing an ostler, barmaid and a general servant. By 1872 Martin Turner was the innkeeper, aged 64 in 1881. George Tabner had taken over between 1885 and 1888 and remained as landlord until the end of the century.

The Mill, built by Ling Robinson, mill-wright of Ballingdon in Essex.

Hartest in 1839

In 1839 the parish of Hartest was surveyed by William Borley of Alpheton. The tithe map and apportionment (1) were drawn up under the terms of the Tithe Commutation Act 1836, whereby money payments were to be substituted for payment of the tithe in kind. In order to assess the 'rent-charge' all the fields and houses were numbered on the map. The apportionment gave details about the owner, occupier, name, use, size and assessment for each piece of land, and also the owner and occupier for each of the houses, including those that were not subject to tithe payment.

From this very comprehensive information we have been able to draw maps showing the areas owned by major land ownders; the areas held by the major land occupiers; the field pattern and land use in 1839. We have also produced maps showing the major land occupiers, the field pattern and land use in 1984, both for comparison and as a record for the future.

The list of house occupiers in 1839 records only the name of one of the families living in each building, other families are indicated by a number. Thus at tithe number 424, in Ballingdon Yard, we find 'John Griggs and two others'. The 1841 Census Returns (2) has been used to provide details about the named families, the 'others' have been identified from the sequence in which the names were listed. This has revealed the other families in the three cottages with John Griggs, to be those of John Baker and Charles Cutmore.

Because of the two year gap between the tithe and census, we have not been able to re-populate all the houses. For example in 1839 number 371, on the east side of the green, was occupied by Charles Went and three others. By 1841 Charles had moved to the west side and there was only one unlocated family, that of Abraham Cater, who could be placed in the four family tenement. Any uncertain locations have been prefixed in the list with a question-mark.

Because of the difficulty of reproducing the whole tithe map so that the original numbers could still be read, we have only carried out this analysis for the central area.

LAND OWNERS HAVING OVER 100 ACRES IN 1839

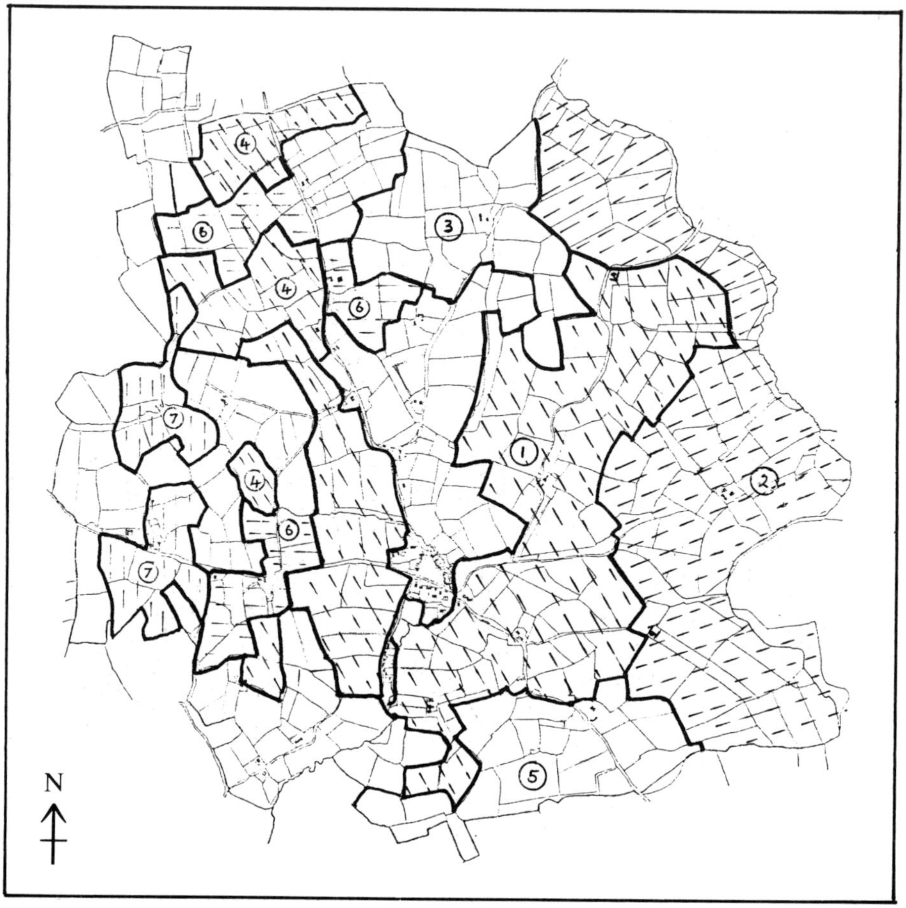

1.	George Weller Poley	477 acres
2.	Thomas Hallifax	360 acres
3.	Col. Acklom	125 acres
4.	John Dickerson	124 acres
5.	Robert Spencer	106 acres
6.	Rev. Henry Mears	102 acres
7.	Hannah King	102 acres

MAJOR LAND OCCUPIERS IN 1839

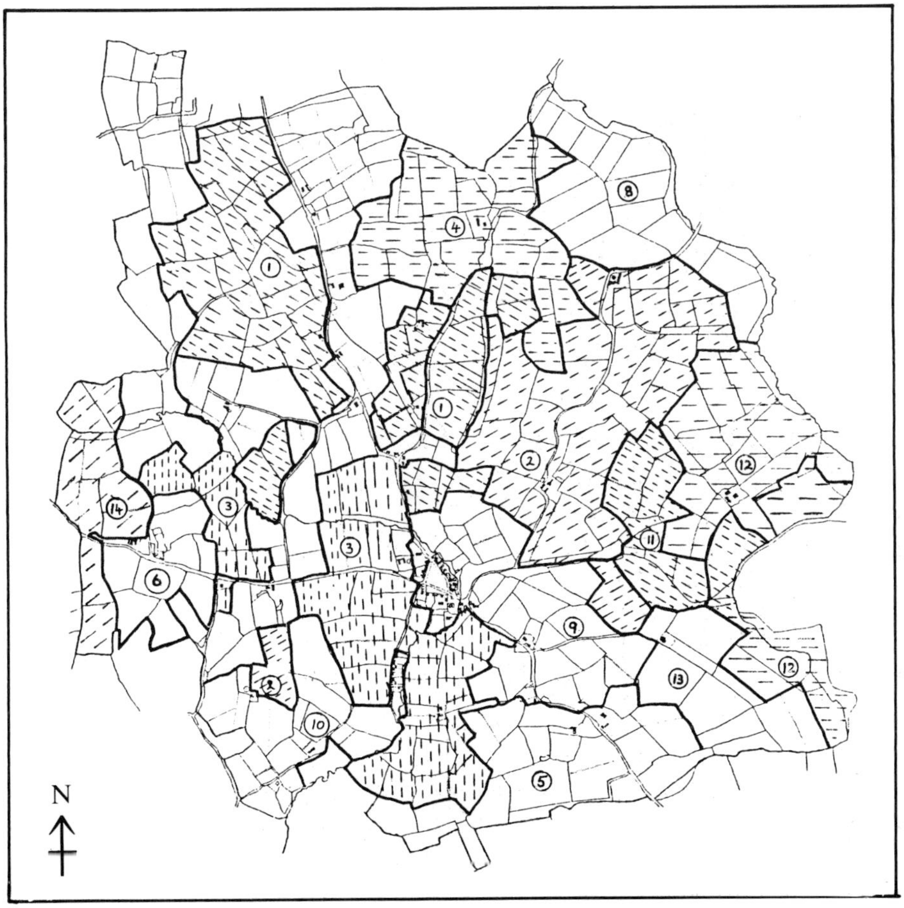

1.	John Dickerson: Burnthouse, Warrens, and Vallence Farms	242 acres
2.	John Nice: Kew Gardens and Cooks Farms	224 acres
3.	Edward Harvey: Place and Brickhouse Farms	178 acres
4.	George Coe: Longs Farm	125 acres
5.	Robert Spencer: Fosters and Cawstons Farms	106 acres
6.	Robert Heywood: Mill End Farm	101 acres
7.	Thomas Abbot: Rivetts Hall Farm	92 acres
8.	John Wymark: Walgraves Farm	81 acres
9.	John Clarke: Hill Farm	79 acres
10.	William Bray: The Mill and Townsend Farm	71 acres
11.	James Debenham: Belchamps Farm	64 acres
12.	Thomas Hallifax: Chadacre Hall	63 acres
13.	Benjamin Pettitt: Lords Farm	63 acres
14.	James Jackson: Mile End Farm	61 acres

LAND HOLDINGS IN 1839

LANDOWNERS IN 1839

	acres	roods	perches
Poley George Weller	477	3	38
Hallifax Thomas	360	3	26
Acklom Colnl. R.E.	125	0	31
Dickerson John	124	0	15
Spencer Robert	106	3	34
Mears Revd. Henry	102	3	30
King Hannah	102	1	1
Jackson John, Sparke James, and Holmes Joseph Hanby	64	3	13
Constable Abraham	61	3	34
King Benjamin	57	3	9
Bevan Robert	44	2	37
Trustees of Spark's Charity	39	1	4
Wallis Revd. William	34	3	20
Jackson James, senr.	34	1	11
Cawston William	27	1	0
Maddy Revd. John, D. D. (Glebe)	25	2	29
Flatt John	21	0	24
Mulley Abraham	19	0	13
Pawsey John	17	1	20
Baynton Stephen	16	1	1
Bray William	11	3	10
Rainow Mary	10	0	22
Trustees to Melford Hospital	10	1	12
Jackson James, junr.	9	3	26
Shave Henry	5	0	16
Garnham George	3	0	32
Bloomfield Rev. James	1	3	29
Candler Samuel	0	2	29
Bradnam John	0	2	4
Joslin John	0	1	37

FARMS AND ACREAGES IN 1839

	acres	roods	perches
Cooks	152	1	10
Longs	125	0	31
Cawstons and Fosters	106	3	34
Mill End	101	1	5
Rivets	96	2	30
Brickhouse	85	0	3
Walgraves	81	0	6
Burnthouse	74	2	1
Kew Gardens	72	0	2
Belchamps	64	0	28
Lords	63	2	29
Hill	63	1	20
Mile End	61	3	34
Townsend	57	3	9
Vallence	57	1	29
Place	54	1	23
Charity	39	1	4
Pickles	34	1	11
Pear Tree	26	2	0
Wisnage	19	0	13
Hartest Place	14	3	34
Warrens	13	2	28
Mill	11	3	10
Tan Office	4	0	18

Details taken from the Tithe Apportionment 1839.

FIELD PATTERN AND LAND USE IN 1839

Roads, waste, Cottages, River, Glebe and Green: 75 acres.

MAJOR LAND OCCUPIERS IN 1984

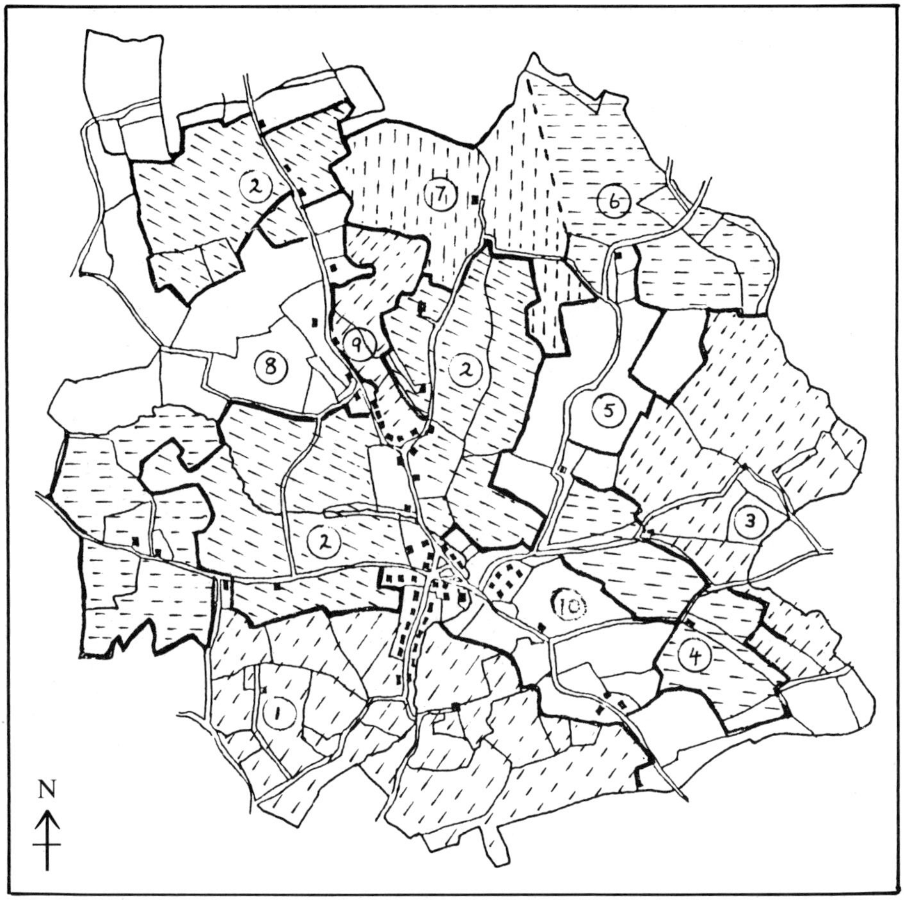

1. Weller Poley Estate
2. Ernie Pask
3. Chadacre
4. Lords Farm
5. John Truin
6. Robin Dennis-Jones
7. Arthur Bird
8. Roy Laflin
9. Cliff White
10. Jack Ince

This list is not arranged in order of acreage.

FIELD PATTERN AND LAND USE IN 1984

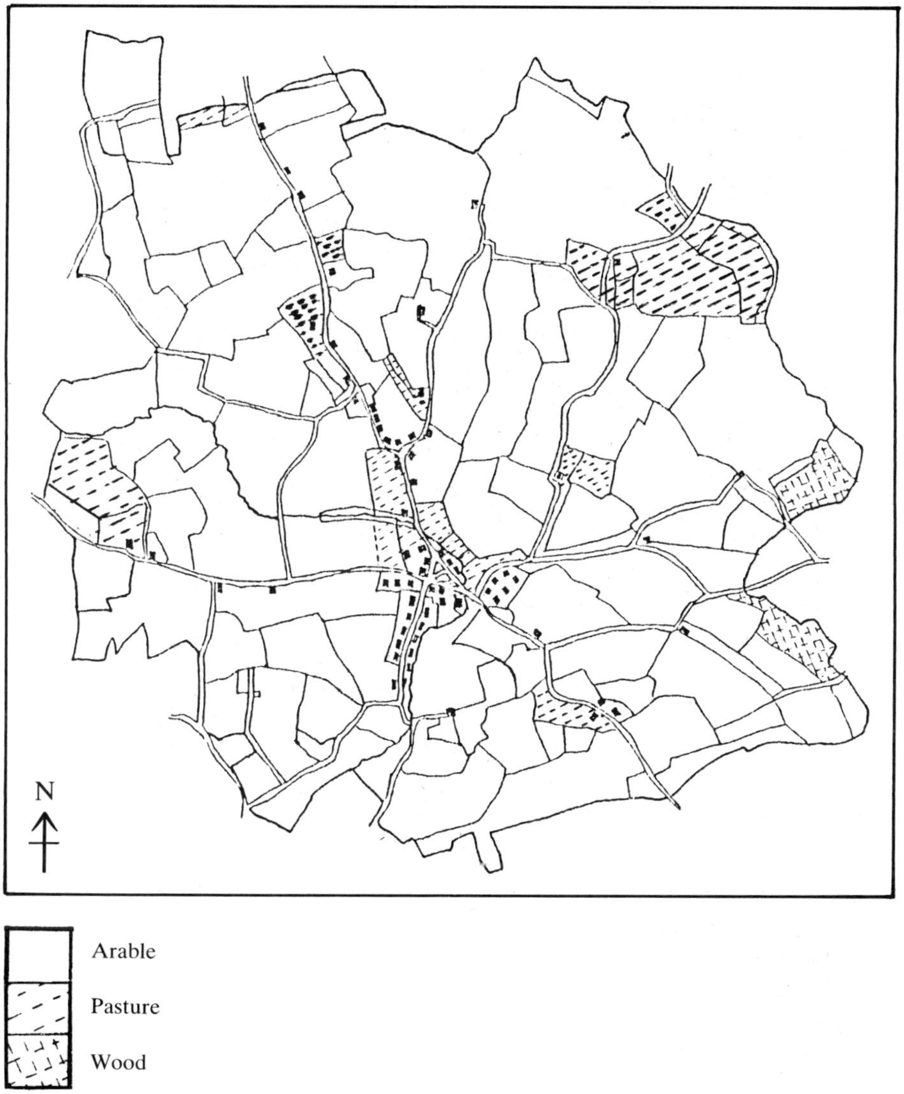

Hartest Green in 1839.

House Occupiers in 1839

The Green: east side

377 John Kimmis in 1839, he had moved to Belchamps Farm Cottage by 1841, he was Parish Clerk and Shoemaker with a wife and four children.

376 Elizabeth Colt, independent, aged 85, daughter and a lodger

375 Frederick Everard, farrier, aged 25, wife, child and two lodgers.
Thomas Jackson, carpenter, aged 45, wife, four children and father.

374 James Bocock, grocer, aged 40, wife, two children, a servant and two lodgers.

373 George Turpin, confectioner, aged 37, and wife.
Harriet Britten, governess of private school, aged 40, thirteen boarding pupils, a servant and a lodger.

?John Cawston, glazier, aged 43, wife, child and a lodger
?George Griggs, baker, aged 30, wife, three children and a servant

371 ?Abraham Cater, independent, aged 80, and wife.

369 William Jackaman, bricklayer, aged 64, wife and child.

367 Robert Debenham, blacksmith, aged 34, wife and two children.
Joseph Grindley, blacksmith, aged 35, and one child.

366 Robert Pettitt, bricklayer, aged 29, wife and three children.

365 Elizabeth Evered, independent, aged 70, and four children

364 William Cawston in 1839, Alfred Cawston in 1841, butcher, aged 30, wife, child, one servant and a lodger.

363 George Cadge, builder, aged 44, wife and two children.
John Case, independent, aged 40, wife, two children and two servants.

The Duddery

372 Isaac Snazell, carrier, aged 60, wife and five children.
William Jeffery, independent, aged 70, and wife.

362 William Pettitt, agricultural labourer, aged 45, wife and three children

361 Elizabeth Wright, independent, aged 55.
James Pettitt, carpenter, aged 70
William Brabrook, agricultural labourer, aged 27, wife and four children.

Pence Green

420 Richard Albon, blacksmith, aged 36, wife, two children and brother.
Elizabeth Pettitt, independent, aged 58, one child

421 Stephen Baynton, independent, aged 60, and wife.

423 George Boreham, harness-maker, aged 50, wife and five children

Ballingdon Yard

422 John Ince, carpenter, aged 35, wife and three children
Noah Debenham, shoemaker, aged 40, three children and lodger
John Seeley, agricultural labourer, aged 25, and wife.

424 John Griggs, agricultural labourer, aged 35, wife and two children.
John Baker, agricultural labourer, aged 39, wife and five children and a lodger.
Charles Cutmore, agricultural labourer, aged 30, wife and two children.

The Green: south side

418 Samuel Crisp, schoolmaster, aged 56, wife, five children and a servant.
?Ann Barrell, independent, aged 56

Church ?Hannah Coe, independent aged 80, and two lodgers
Cottage ?Ellen Brabrook, independent, aged 60, and a lodger.

416 Rev. Edward Butts, Rector, aged 45, wife, seven children and seven servants.

415 William Maxim, publican, aged 40, wife, five children and two servants

414 John Adams, shoemaker, aged 65, wife and four children.

413 William Smith, agricultural labourer, aged 55, and five children

412 John Beeton, independent, aged 85, and son.
Sarah Prigg, independent, aged 90, and a lodger.
Hannah Serjeant, independent, aged 45 and one child.

410 Joseph Maxim, agricultural labourer, aged 55, wife and seven children.
Ebenezer Knopp, shoemaker, aged 52, wife and six children.

411 John Dickerson, farmer, aged 50, wife, two children and two servants.
John Smith, Carpenter, aged 50, wife and four lodgers.

The Green: west side

382 Henry Coote, gardener, aged 30, wife and three children.
Samuel Ince, carpenter, aged 40, wife and three children.

380 Richard Kent, tailor, aged 40, wife, child and mother.
Thomas Pope, carpenter, aged 40, wife, seven children, mother and a lodger.
Charles West, tea dealer, aged 75, and wife.

379 ?Robert Prigg, cooper, aged 40 and one child.

378 James Jeffery, woolcarder, aged 55, and wife.
Thomas Ward, wheelwright, aged 61 and wife
George Garwood, agricultural labourer, aged 25, wife and two children

336 George King, surgeon, aged 44, wife, three servants and two lodgers.
?Frederick Esterford, shoemaker, aged 35, wife and five children.

The ages of the occupants are as recorded in the 1841 census.

The Green, c.1910: showing William Garrard's butchers shop. He had taken over the business business from George Cawston c.1902, and was succeeded by Reginald Basham in 1926.

Hartest in 1844

HARTEST, a pleasant village, in the bosom of a deep valley, 8 miles N. by W. of Sudbury, and 7 miles N.E. of Clare, has in its parish 812 souls, and 1964A. 28p. of land, rising in bold undulations, and bounded on the east and west by two rivulets. It anciently belonged to the convent of Ely, and afterwards to the see of Ely, until the 4th of Elizabeth. G. W. Poley, Esq., is now lord of the manor, but a great part of the soil belongs to Thos. Hallifax, Esq., Col. Acklom, Mr R. Spencer, and several smaller owners. The Church (All Saints) is an ancient Gothic fabric, with a tower and five bells, and the benefice is a rectory, valued in the Kings Book at £29 14s.2d., and in 1835, at £652, with the rectory of Boxtead annexed to it, in the patronage of the Crown and incumbency of the Rev. J. Maddy, D.D., of Stansfield. The tithes were commuted, in 1839, for a yearly modus of £611, including the quota on 25A.2R.29P. of glebe. In 1721, THOMAS SPARKE left to the rector of Hartest and certain trustees, a farm, in this parish, of 39A.3R.21P., for charitable uses. The farm is let for £50 a year, out of which the following payments are made, agreeable to the donor's will, viz.,—20s. per annum each to Rede, Brockley, and Hartest, for the ministers and churchwardens of those parishes, as a remuneration for their trouble in examining the accounts of this charity at Easter: and £6 a year for schooling poor children of Brockley. The residue, after payment of a quit-rent, etc., is applied in sending poor children of Hartest to school. In 1808, the Rev. W. W. Poley and others were appointed as new trustees. In 1646, THOMAS WRIGHT left two cottages for the residence of two poor widows not chargeable to the parish; and for their reparation, he charged an adjoining tenement, called Penns, with the yearly payment of 10s. The poor of Hartest have about 25s. yearly from Corder's Charity (see Glemsford) and a fifth part of Poley's Charity (see Boxted).

Albon Richard, blacksmith
Baynton Mr Stephen, Mount
Boreham Geo. saddler & harness mkr
Bray Wm. corn miller // Case Mr John
Butts Rev Edward Drury, MA. curate, Rectory
Cadge George, builder & wheelwgt
Cawston John, plumber and glazier
Crisp Samuel, free school master
Death Ellen, boarding & day school
Everitt Frederick, farrier
Jageman Wm. bricklayer
King George, surgeon
Leadbeater Hy. Esq. Hartest Lodge
Maxim Joseph, victualler, Bell
Maxim Wm. victualler, Crown
Mears Rev Henry, curate of Rede, Stow Hill
Ranson Wm. plumber and glazier
Sadler James, shopkeeper
Turner Rt. butcher & cattle dealer
Turpin James, baker
Whindread Wm. beerhouse keeper

FARMERS

*are Owners.
Abbott Robert, Rivett's Hall
Bradenham Jno.
Bray Wm.
Cawston Alfred, (and butcher)
Clarke John
Coe George
Debenham Jas.
*Dickerson Jno.
Griggs James
Harvey James Broom, Brick hs
Haywood Robert
Jackson James
Nice Jno. Cook's Farm
Payne Samuel, (and maltster)
*Spencer Robert

GROCERS & DRAPERS

Bocock James
Bannock Thos.

SHOEMAKERS

Adams John
Debenham Jas.
Debenham Noah
Kimmes John
Smith Samuel

TAILORS

Kent Richard
Sturgeon George

CARRIERS

Henry Knopp, to Bury, M. Wed. and Sat, & to Sudbury, Thurs
Isaac Snazell, to Bury, W. & Sat. and to Sudbury, Mon. & Friday

Taken from The Directory of Suffolk, by William White 1844.

Occupations in Hartest 1841-1881

	1841	1851	1861	1871	1881
AGRICULTURE					
Agricultural Labourer	98	133	128	109	102
Bailiff	–	1	4	4	2
Cattle Dealer	–	1	1	–	–
Dairymaid/man	–	–	1	–	1
Dealer	1	1	–	–	2
Farmer	15	12	15	21	15
Farmer's Son	–	–	–	9	3
Gamekeeper	–	–	1	1	1
Hay Dealer	–	1	–	–	–
Miller	5	4	3	3	3
Mole Catcher	–	–	–	–	1
Pig Dealer	–	4	2	–	–
BREWING					
Barmaid	–	1	1	1	–
Beerhouse keeper	–	–	1	–	–
Beer seller	–	–	–	2	1
Brewer	–	–	–	–	2
Innkeeper	2	2	2	2	2
Maltster	1	3	–	–	1
EDUCATION					
School Teacher (Female)	1	1	5	5	4
School Teacher (Male)	2	2	–	1	1
Governess	2	–	–	–	1
Scholar	–	109	115	138	184
INDEPENDENT MEANS					
Annuitant/Independant	60	4	1	7	–
No Occupation	–	–	–	12	15
Magistrate	–	–	–	–	1
Proprietor of Houses/Land	–	5	–	–	–

	1841	1851	1861	1871	1881
INDUSTRY					
Hairweaver/server/dresser	–	6	3	–	–
Silk Worker	–	6	3	–	–
Silk Weaver	–	–	–	2	–
Strawplaiter	–	18	2	–	–
Weaver	–	–	–	–	1
Woolworker	1	2	5	–	–
PAUPERS/PENSIONERS					
Chelsea/Greenwich Pensioner	–	1	2	2	2
Pauper	–	55	–	–	–
PROFESSIONS					
Clergyman	2	2	2	1	1
Congregational Minister	–	–	–	1	1
General Practioner/Surgeon	1	1	1	1	2
Medical Student	–	–	–	–	2
Veterinary Surgeon	–	–	1	1	–
PUBLIC SERVICES					
Excise Officer	1	1	1	–	1
Parish Clerk	–	–	–	1	–
Police Officer	–	–	–	–	1
Post Master/Mistress	–	–	1	1	1
SERVANTS					
Charwoman	–	2	–	3	5
Coachman	–	1	1	–	3
Cook	–	–	–	2	3
Errand Boy	–	7	–	–	1
Footman	–	1	1	–	–
Gardener	2	5	2	2	3
Groom/Ostler	–	2	5	4	3
Housemaid	–	–	–	2	5
Housekeeper	–	5	2	2	3
Kitchenmaid	–	–	–	–	1
Nurse/Nurse Girl	–	5	1	2	3
Parlour Maid	–	–	–	2	–
Servant (Male)	19	4	–	2	1
Servant (Female)	30	26	–	15	15

	1841	1851	1861	1871	1881
TRADES AND SERVICES					
Baker	1	1	2	3	2
Baker's Boy	–	–	–	2	1
Blacksmith	4	4	5	4	2
Bricklayer	5	7	5	8	5
Brickmaker	3	–	–	–	–
Builder	1	–	1	–	1
Butcher	4	2	3	3	4
Carpenter	10	3	10	6	9
Carrier	1	1	3	–	1
Chimney Sweep	–	2	2	1	2
Confectioner	1	–	–	–	–
Cooper	1	–	–	–	–
Dress Maker/Seamstress	–	8	10	7	6
Glazier	2	–	–	4	2
Glover	–	1	–	–	–
Grocer/Draper	2	2	3	4	4
Harnessmaker/Saddler	1	2	1	2	2
Laundress	–	7	6	5	2
Marine Store Dealer	–	–	1	–	–
Milk Seller	–	–	–	1	–
Milliner	–	1	1	–	–
Organ Builder	–	–	–	1	1
Painter	–	–	–	2	1
Photographic Artist	–	–	2	–	–
Plumber	–	2	3	6	2
Rat Catcher	–	2	1	–	1
Sawyer	–	1	1	2	2
Shoemaker	10	13	–	8	4
Shopman	1	4	–	1	–
Tailor	5	3	3	3	1
Tea Dealer	1	–	–	–	–
Thatcher	3	4	2	–	–
Wheelwright	4	4	4	4	3

All these details have been taken from the Census Returns.

Map 9: Suffolk birthplaces of Hartest residents in 1851.
Details taken from the Census Return.

Map 10: Suffolk birthplaces of Hartest residents in 1881.
Details taken from the Census Return.

Ernest Pask (1873–1945), Abner Griggs (1864–1919), and William Willoughby (1871–1948), in Mill Field, c.1904.

The Restoration of the Church 1879-80

At a Vestry meeting on 14 January 1879 the Rev. Arthur Packer, Rector of Hartest and Boxted, proposed '. . . that plans should be adopted for restoring and repairing the parish church . . .' (1). He promised to raise £400 on condition that the parish contributed £150 towards the work. The Vestry responded by granting a voluntary rate of one shilling in the pound for two years.

Later meetings appointed Mr John Drayton Wyatt a London architect, and invited Mr Thomas Cadge of Hartest to submit a tender for the restoration. The 1881 census shows that he lived on the Green and had twenty-seven men and two boys in his employment.

In June plans and specifications, amounting to £1,500 were submitted to the Chancellor of the Diocese of Ely and in July a faculty was granted. From these documents, it is clear that the south wall of the lady chapel required rebuilding as it was '. . . so much thrust out of the perpendicular, and cracked, so as to be becoming dangerous, the foundations having apparently yielded to the pressure of the chancel-arch, and side arch continuation. These latter arches are displaced in their form, and their masonry, and will have to be taken down and rebuilt. The Chancel Arch is now in a critical state and only kept up by the assistance of unsightly shoring underneath . . .' The chancel arch, lady chapel arch and the south wall were to be rebuilt '. . . according to the original design . . .' (2).

At the same time the opportunity was taken to 'modernise' the interior of the church. In the chancel the plaster ceiling was removed and the present oak roof constructed; two lancet windows above the communion table were replaced by the five-light east window; the table with its three sided communion rail was removed, and the present arrangement substituted. This rail could well have been 17th century and similar to that surviving at Boxted. Behind the table, and filling the width of the church on wooden boards were the Lord's Prayer, Creed and Ten Commandments, and these were also removed.

In the nave, the gallery across the west end was removed. This had probably been originally constructed for singers and musicians. David Davy in 1831, described it as '. . . housing a small organ . . .' above which were the Royal Arms (3). Beneath it stood the font '. . . carved with bunches of leaves . . .' which was the replacement for the one removed in the Civil War. This in turn was now replaced by the present font. The roof had been hidden by a flat plaster ceiling, which was removed and the roof restored on the lines of the 17th century original. The 17th century pulpit, described in 1831 as being painted '. . . a yellowish colour . . .' was cleaned and reset on a new base.

Other repairs were the blocking up of the east window of the north chapel, and a small window in the south clerestory of the nave. This latter is probably the lancet window now in the south wall of the vestry.

Throughout the church the benches, described in 1831, as '. . . deal and common' were replaced. When the Suffolk Institute of Archaeology visited the church in 1859 the interior was described in the following words '. . . there were pews of every kind, but ugly alike, from the variety termed sleeping boxes, to one with a lumbering canopy, the latter having been designed we believe, by an old gentleman who suffered from the cold!' (4). Materials from these benches were re-used in the north aisle, for children's seats in the lady chapel, and the 'ancient tracery panelling' re-used in the front seat of the nave.

The brick floors were replaced with quarry and glazed tiles. The walls must have been whitewashed, as in 1831 the bases and capitals of the arcades were painted bright blue.

In 1859 the writer commented that '. . . various interesting features of the sacred edifice are either so mutilated, changed or hidden, that few churches present so wide a field for any attempt at even decent restoration.' The eventual restoration in 1879-80 like many others was achieved at a great loss to posterity. In that one period of 'improvement' 14th century lancet windows; 16th century benches; 17th century communion rails and font; 18th century gallery, organ and royal arms were all 'restored' away.

By September 1880, when the church was re-opened for worship, the present internal arrangement had been created. The tower was repaired and both porches refaced and restored in 1890.

The Green, c.1904: showing the Chapel, before the new windows were inserted in 1906, and John Crickmores shop. He was a grocer, draper, wine and spirits merchant, taking over the business from William Crow in the early 1890s, and by 1908 had gone into partnership with Edward Savage.

The Congregationalists

The earliest record of Independent or Congregational services being held in Hartest was 1815, when the house of Jeremiah Humm, near the Bell Inn, was licensed for worship (1). Although both the Methodists and Baptists held house services in the village, only the Congregationalists were able to establish a 'church' with a pastor, members and a chapel building.

The Rev John Rutter, Minister of Stansfield Congregational Church was the prime mover behind the formation of a church at Hartest. In 1843 he appointed Robert Pawsey of Lidgate as an evangelist serving the parishes of Stradishall, Depden, Chedburgh, Chevington, Rede, Hartest, Somerton and Hawkedon (2).

In the 1840s and 1850s services were held either in houses, or on the green, which were conducted by local pastors including Rev John Rutter and Mr Manning Prentice of Stowmarket. In 1864 the latter purchased some cottages on the green, which were converted into a chapel and a minister's residence at the cost of £364. The chapel opened for worship on Sunday 15 June 1864.

In March 1867 the worshippers decided to form themselves into a 'church' in membership with the Suffolk Congregational Association (3). This meant the congregation at Hartest could now become church members, appoint a pastor and receive the Sacraments. The Rev J. P. Bake was appointed the first minister and a list of members entered into the Church Book. The founding members were four men, ten women and Mr and Mrs Bake. The 1871 Census has been used where possible, to provide details about the members' occupations and ages in 1867. These facts have been added to the list of names in order to show the socio-economic composition of the church.

William Harvey aged 31 farmer and miller employing 6 men; his wife Eliza aged 29, both of whom transferred their membership from Stanstead to Hartest: their domestic servant Susan Pannell aged 37; Charles Colson aged 41, farmer of Tan Office Farm, who employed one man and two boys on his 62 acres; Mrs Fanny Clarke aged 81, farmer of Clarke's Farm, who employed three men and a boy on her 63 acres; Mrs Mary Spencer aged 80, farmer, of Spencers Farm who employed four men and three boys on 115 acres; Mary Ann Evered wife of an agricultural labourer; Agnes Jackson aged 23, laundress and wife of James Jackson, Plumber and Glazier; Mrs Gowers and Mrs Debenhamm all of Hartest; Sophia Harvey aged 58 and her son John aged 22, both of Park Farm Boxted, where they employed five men and three boys on 130 acres; and finally Mr and Mrs William Willis of Shimpling.

All the members covenanted and promised '. . . this day, in the strength of Divine Grace, to walk henceforth, in the commandments of our Lord Jesus Christ; and we agree to submit to the order and discipline observed in Congregational Churches . . .' (4).

The Rev J. P. Bake remained at Hartest until 1868, and in December Rev James Ellis became the minister, serving the church until July 1871. Rev Ellis, aged 30 in 1871, lodged at the home of another church member Mrs Agnes Jackson and her husband James, who was to become a member himself in 1876. During the pastorate of Rev Ellis no new members joined the church, and six of the founder members moved away from Hartest.

Although the membership remained small, large numbers of adults and children attended the services. In October 1871 for example 130 people came to a 'Tea Meeting' and in the same month a Sunday School opened with 34 children and four teachers.

Between 1871 and 1876 the following became members, Alfred Sturgeon aged 35, master tailor; his wife Fanny aged 44; William Pask aged 28, sawyer; Sarah Knapp aged 32, wife of an agricultural labourer; Rosa Cadge aged 19, daughter of Thomas Cadge, builder and farmer; Mary Ann Ginn aged 56, a seamstress and her daughter Sarah Ann aged 27, both of Potash cottages; Mrs Griggs; Joseph Jackson aged 51, plumber and glazier; Job Ginn aged 36, sawyer; Henry Hinds aged 53, blacksmith, Ada Cook aged 20, daughter of Henry Cook, carpenter; and finally Mary Ann Payne aged 24, daughter of John Payne, an agricultural labourer.

By 1876 the number of Sunday School pupils had risen to 96, and the number of teachers to sixteen. The latter included members of the following families, Dye, Ginn, Hinds, Jackson, Knapp, Maxim, Pask, Payne, Smith, Steed and Sturgeon.

Mr William Pask became the Church Treasurer, and from 1879 lived in the Manse, where he opened a shop in the front room and operated his carrier's service. His wife Hannah (née Ginn) never became a member of the church, and eventually both she and their children attended the Brethren meeting.

From 1877 to 1894 there were only two years when minutes of church business had been recorded. It seems that in the 1880s everything was in decline. In 1883 the Sunday School was in need of 'resuscitation' and might actually have ceased to function. There had been no resident minister or pastor since about 1877 and the membership by 1884 was reduced to twelve. The members were William Harvey aged 48, a member since 1867, miller, brewer and farmer of 107 acres at Hartest Mill; his wife Eliza aged 45, a member since 1867; William Pask aged 41, now a carrier and shopkeeper, a member since 1871; Ada Cook aged 25, a member since 1875; Henry Hinds aged 59, blacksmith, a member since 1876; Thomas Farthing aged 67, carpenter; Henry Coote aged 38, a carpenter, and his wife Clara aged 41, these last three became members after 1877; Mr and Mrs J Hayward and Mr and Mrs Wright seem to have become members since 1881.

In May 1890 Mr C. Prentice came to live at Hartest, in order to take on the pastorate of the church and to sell Bibles and religious books in the surrounding villages. The church now had a resident pastor for the first time since 1877. The congregation increased in that year from eight to fifty people.

Mr Prentice was dismissed in October 1891 and his place taken by Mr John Poulson, who remained as pastor until 1933. The Church Book records that at the time of Mr Poulson's appointment 'there was no recognised church in Hartest' (5). In April 1894 it was decided to '. . . Reform the church, to institute the Sacrament of the Lords Supper, and to hold church meetings . . .' (6). The six other members in 1894 were, William and Eliza Harvey, Thomas Farthing, William Pask, Henry and Clara Coote.

In 1906 the Chapel was restored, and new windows inserted, the cost being raised by voluntary contributions.

Following the resignation of Mr Poulson in 1933, Mr Ben Watson became pastor, at a salary of £52 a year, and remained until 1939. In 1941 Rev E. A. Chilvers accepted the pastorate and over 150 people attended his induction service in April 1942. He remained at Hartest until his death in 1961.

The Chapel closed on 20 July 1980, the final service being conducted by Rev Colin Evan, the Moderator of the Eastern Province of the United Reformed Church. In May 1981 the building was sold for conversion into a dwelling, which was offered for sale in April 1982.

Ministers and Pastors of the Congregational Church

1864–67	Rev. John Rutter and Mr Manning Prentice had oversight
1867–68	Rev. J. P. Bake
1868–71	Rev. James Ellis
1871–72	Rev. W. S. Laukford
1872–73	Rev. C. Slater
1874–77	Mr Fulcher
1877–90	Gap in the records
1890	Mr C. Prentice
1891–1933	Mr John Poulson
1934–39	Mr J. B. Watson
1941–61	Rev. E. A. Chilvers
1961–80	Supply preachers
1980	Closed

The Green, c.1910; showing the wheelwrights shop and the saw pit.

The Green, c.1926: notice the two char-a-banc by the wheelwright's shop; the restored 'Church Cottage'; and the dramatic height of Hill Farm above the Green.

The Plymouth Brethren

The Plymouth, or Christian, Brethren do not keep detailed records of their services and activities. Each meeting or assembly is a self governing body, and there is no central organisation to collate and hold records. Therefore the history of an assembly has to be based on oral evidence and any legal documents relating to the Trustees of the Gospel Hall.

The earliest recorded reference to a meeting at Hartest occurs in 1890 when the Gospel Room was licensed for marriages. Before then services were held in Potash Cottages, the home of Mary Ann Ginn and her daughter Sarah, and subsequently at the Club Room of the Bell. The first wedding was in May 1900 when May Pask, daughter of William who lived at the Congregational Manse, married Rev J. Shildrick a Baptist Minister (1).

Some time before 1890 William Crow, Grocer and Draper, purchased the former Wrights Almshouses on Hartest Hill, and had them converted into a Gospel Room, which on his death in 1910 was sold to nine Trustees. The property seems originally to have been three cottages, two of which, including the yard between them, became the Gospel Room, and the third was left as a dwelling.

The Trustees were James Ashby of Cricklewood, evangelist; John Bradnam, gardener; Clement Ellingham, baker; Charles and George Honeywood, farmers, all residing in Hartest; George Hibble, carpenter; George Goldsmith and Henry Mortlock, agricultural labourers, all of Shimpling. James Ashby had done much to help establish the meeting by holding annual tent meetings on the village green.

The Trust deed specified both how the building was to be used, and the doctrine of the Brethren. The Gospel Room was '. . . to be used and occupied for the purpose of holding meetings for the worship of God, for the purpose of remembering the Lord Jesus Christ in the Breaking of Bread on the first day of every week, and for the preaching and expounding of the Word of God both for adults and children, and generally for any purpose which shall be calculated to promote the diffusion and practice of the truths and doctrines contained in the Holy Scriptures and particularly the doctrines following viz:– The Trinity in Unity of God; the incarnation of the Son of God; the personality of the Holy Ghost; the plenary inspiration of the Holy Scriptures; the ruin and depravity of man; the necessity for repentance and regeneration and redemption justification by faith; the Sovereignty of God and the reponsibility of man; the eternal blessedness of the redeemed and the eternal punishment of the lost; but so that in such meetings the only baptism to be taught and practised shall be that by immersion upon confession of individual faith in the Lord Jesus Christ'.

Between the wars, the afternoon Sunday School was attended by about 100 children. Prize giving was held at Christmas and a 'treat' to Walton-on-the-Naze in the Summer. During the war the 'treats' were held at Hill Farm or on

Maddys Meadow. In the late 1940s the trips to Walton started again. The children were given bags of threepenny bits to spend, and the day ended with a tea of bread-and-butter and shrimps.

For many years the resident evangelist was Mr Edwin Warnock of Hill Farm. The meeting also helped to support the Oliver family as missionaries in India, and who made Hartest their home when in England.

The numbers attending the meeting declined in the 1960s and the final service at the Gospel Room was held in November 1977. The congregation numbered only five, including Mr John Bradnam one of the original Trustees.

The building was sold and re-converted into a house in 1982.

Hartest Hill showing the Gospel Hall and Hill Farm.

The Row, c.1980: showing Oscar H Ince, grocer and draper outside his shop; notice one window displays grocery items, the other drapery.

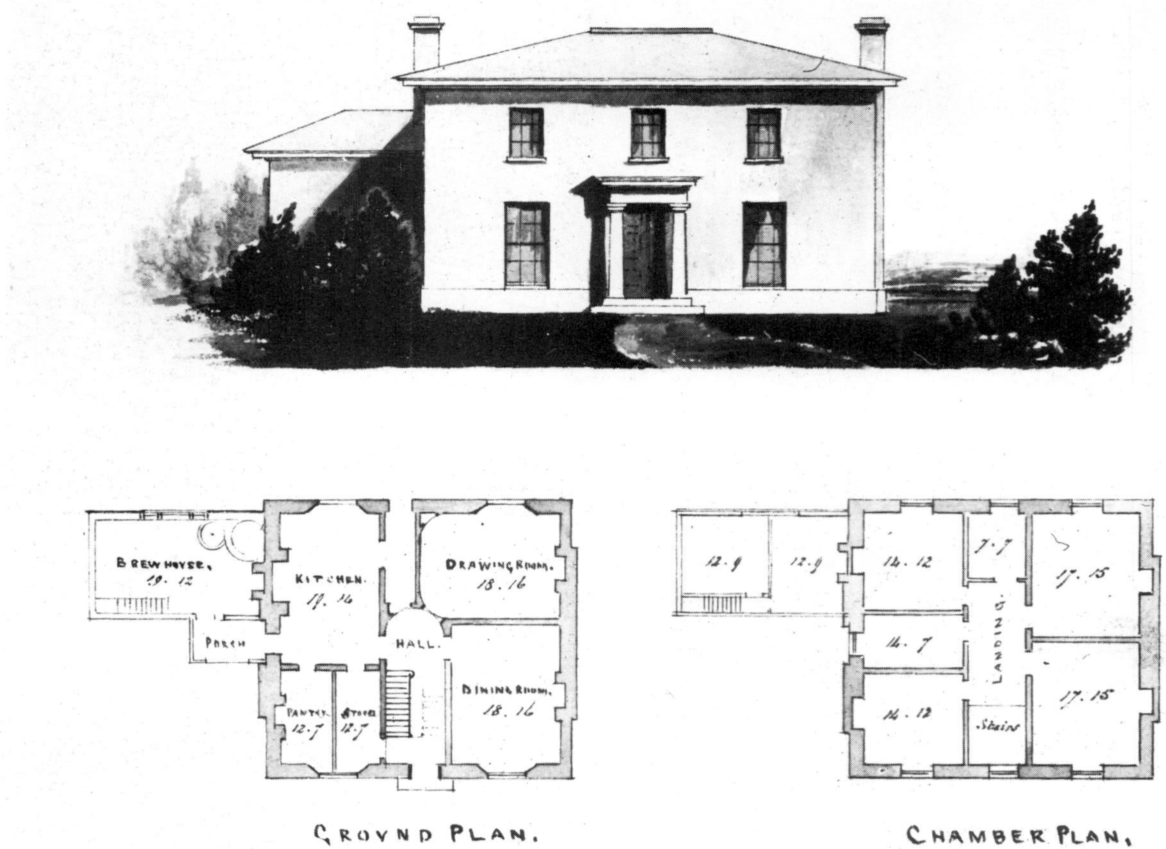

Plans and elevation for Hartest Rectory 1821.

The Rectory

The earliest reference to a Rectory or Parsonage in Hartest occurs in the Glebe Terrier of 1613, when it is described as 'The parsonage Howse, Backehowse, barn & Carthouse with the Gardens and yardes, by estimacion one Acre.' (1).

The abuttals recorded in the Terrier of 1638, show the Parsonage to have stood on the same site as the present Regency building '. . . the Rectory house with a backhouse a little distant from the same, (? a detached kitchen or storehouse), with a very large barne & a stable with the yardes and gardens conteyning together about a rood of ground . . .' (2). The site abutted north on the churchyard and a 'long peece of ground' (the driveway to the Rectory), east on the river, and west on Banton Pasture which in later documents was described as land belonging to Hartest Hall.

In 1821 plans and specifications were drawn up for building the present Rectory. The architect employed by the Bishop of Ely was Mark Grayston Thompson of Dedham in Essex. He reported to the Bishop that he found the '. . . Rectory house and the offices thereto belonging in a very decayed state, quite unfit for the residence of the Rector of the said Rectory, and requiring to be taken down and rebuilt (3). The cost of the new building, allowing for the sale of old materials was £1,420.

Rev. Arthur Packer: Rector of Hartest and Boxted 1879–1906.

A terrier of the parsonage houses and gleebe lands belonging to the rectory of the parish of Hartest in the sayd Countie made & taken upon the twelveth day of September Anno Domini 1638 and in the 14th yeare of the reigne of our soveraigne lord Charles now King of England, Scotland, France etc: by Frederick Gibb Clerke Rector of the sayd parish and James Sparke and John Underwood Church wardens there as Followeth:

Inpremis the Rectory howse with a backhouse a little distant from the same with a very large barne & stable with the yards and garden conteyning togither about a rood of ground and are scituate & doe ley between the Churchyard of Hartest aforesayd in most part and the long peece of ground hereunder next abuttalled in some part on the part of the north & the little river there running from Hartest towards Boxted on the est part & the pasture called Banton on the west part.

Item one longe peece of ground used for a way to the sayd Rectory house conteyning by estemacon one rood of ground lying betweene the Churchyard aforesayd on the Est part & the sayd pasture Called banton on the west part one head thereof abutting upon the Rectory house aforesayd toward the south & the other head upon the greene called Hartest greene & upon the Cottage called the Almshouse towards the north.

Item three Closes of land & pasture lying togither & Conteyning by estimacon one & twenty acres & three roods leying between the land belonging to the Church of Boxted in part & the lands of John Hayward in part on the south part & the messuage & lands of the sayd John Hayward on the north part the one head thereof abutting upon the land of the sayd John towards the Est & upon the Custimary land late in the tenure of Thomas Palsey deceased in part towards the west togither with a way to & from the sayd three closes by, through,& over the west end of a close of pasture of the sayd John Hayward.

Item one other close of land lying between the Custimary lands late in the tenure of Danyell Copping deceased on the north & est parts and the Kings heigh way leading from Hartest greene towards St Edmunds Bury on the west part and a little lane leading to the land called Kates acer on the South part and doe Conteyning by estimacon fowre acers.

Fred: Gib: Rector

John Underwood)
James Sparke) Churchwardens

SR0(B)E13/4/3.

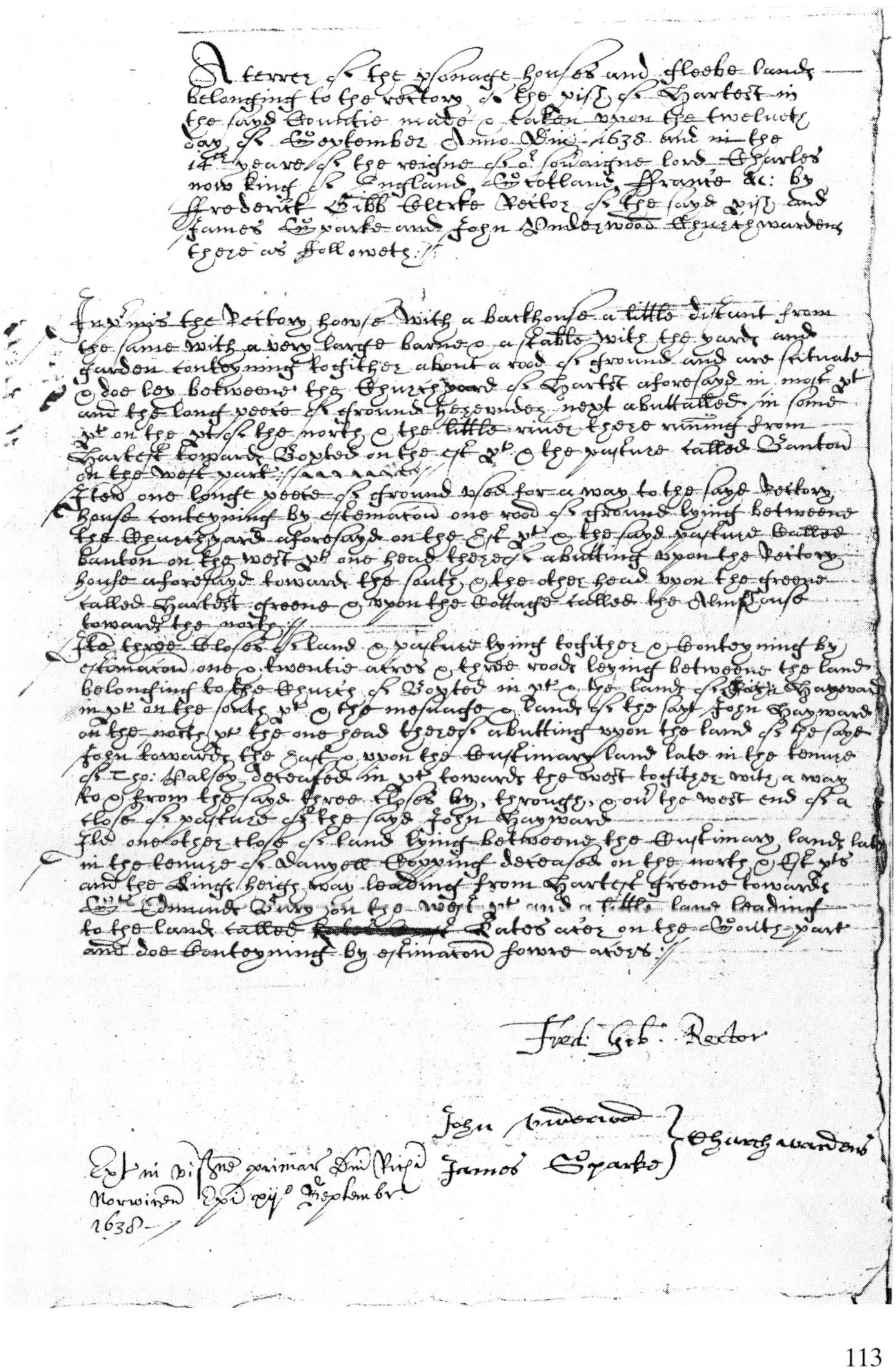

A terrier of the parsonage houses and gleebe lands belonging to the rectory of the parish of Hartest in the sayd Countie made & taken upon the twelveth day of September Anno Dni 1638 and in the 14th yeare of the reigne of o[u]r soveraigne lord Charles now king of England Scotland France &c: by Frederick Gibb Clerke Rector of the sayd parish and James Sparke and John Underwood Churchwardens there as followeth

Imprimis the Rectory house with a backhouse a little distant from the same with a very large barne & a stable with the yard and garden conteyning togither about a rood of ground and are situate & doe lye betweene the Churchyard of Hartest aforesayd in most p[ar]t and the long peece of ground hereunder next abutted in some p[ar]t on the est the north & the little river there running from Hartest toward Boxted on the est p[ar]t & the pasture called Banton on the west part [illegible]

Item one longe peece of ground used for a way to the sayd Rectory house conteyning by estimation one rood of ground lying betweene the Churchyard aforesayd on the Est p[ar]t & the sayd pasture called Banton on the west p[ar]t one head thereof abutting upon the Rectory house aforesayd toward the south & the other head upon the greene called Hartest greene & upon the Cottage called the Almshouse towards the north

Item three closes of land & pasture lying togither & conteyning by estimation one & twentie acres & three roods lying betweene the land belonging to the Church of Boxted in p[ar]t & the land of John Hayward in p[ar]t on the south p[ar]t & the mesuage & land of the sayd John Hayward on the north p[ar]t the one head thereof abutting upon the land of the sayd John towards the east & upon the Customary land late in the tenure of Tho: Walson deceased in p[ar]t towards the west togither with a way to & from the sayd three closes by, through, & on the west end of a close of pasture of the sayd John Hayward

Item one other close of land lying betweene the Customary land late in the tenure of Daniell Cowing deceased on the north & est p[ar]ts and the Kings highway leading from Hartest greene towards Mr Edmund Wyes on the west p[ar]t and a little lane leading to the land called Kates acre on the South part and doe conteyning by estimation fowre acres

Fred: Gib: Rector

John Underwood }
James Sparke } Churchwardens

Ext in visitac[i]one primar[ia] D[omi]ni Rich[ar]d Norwicen Ep[iscop]i xij° Septembr 1638

Group outside the School, c.1912.

School Gardening Class 1915.
Front Row; left to right: —— Baker, Percy Cadge, Jack Pask, Stanley Honeywood, Frederick Payne, Frederick Baker.
Back Row: Quality Carsbolt, Edward Hines, Stanley Pask, Edward Osborne, Arthur Younges, Ernest Pask, Edward Pettitt.

Schools in Hartest

The earliest mention of education in Hartest was 1567, when Alice Gardiner bequeathed 5s. 'If they make a school house in Hartest . . .' (1). However, there is no evidence to show whether or not any school was eventually built.

In the early 18th century there seem to have been at least two schools in Hartest. A Charity School connected with the S.P.C.K. was opened in 1708 for the instruction of 32 boys who were taught to 'Read, Write and the Catechism, and also the Grounds of Arithmetic . . .' (2). Two years later eight boys from Somerton were attending the school, which was described as 'increasing daily'. The Schoolmaster who had '. . . the Art of teaching above the common sort . . .' was paid 2s. 6d. a quarter for each child. Subscriptions for the support of the school in 1710 amounted to £262 and the Master of St John's College Cambridge gave Mr Harrison, of Stow Hill House, and steward of the school, £30 for clothing the forty boys (3).

Anthony Oakley, a wealthy property owner in Hartest, in 1713 bequeathed £10 a year '. . . towards the erecting of a School, and for educating of six boys, five out of this parish and one out of Somerton . . . to be taught by the Curate to the Rector of Hartest' (4).

In 1721 Thomas Sparke of Rougham, gentleman, gave a house and 40 acres (later known as Charity Farm) to provide an annual income for the '. . . buying of books and the schooling of poor children of and within the said parish of Hartest . . .' (5). There is no evidence to indicate whether the school taught by the Curate was ever started. Therefore it is most probable that the Sparke's Charity endowment was used to support the earlier Charity School.

There is no further evidence relating to the school in the 18th century. But in the 19th century much can be gleaned from the Sparke's Charity Account Book (6), local directories and Parliamentary Enquiries into educational provisions.

In 1818 Hartest had 'several day schools'; a school for 20-30 children supported by Sparke's Charity; and a Sunday School with 67 children, which was supported by the parish (7).

The children attending the Charity or Free School were selected by the Rector of Hartest. They were first taught reading, for which the schoolmaster received 4s. 6d. a quarter for each child, and then reading, writing and arithmetic, for which he received 6s. 6d. from the Charity. Other children also attended the school, their parents paying the master for their education. For example in 1833 the school had 29 charity and 44 fee-paying pupils.

The Charity children were divided into 'readers' and 'writers' and a list of their names recorded in the Account Book each year. From these lists it has been possible to discover at what age the children started school, how long they were 'readers' and 'writers' and the length of their school life. A sample study of those children at school in 1841 shows that they started school from between two and eleven years old: 5% started at 2 years old; 9.7% at 3 years; 12.2% at 4; 31.2% at 5; 5% at 6; 7.3% at 7; 7.3% at 8; 5% at 9; 5% at 10; and 5% at 11 years of age. No ages could be determined for a further 7.3% of the sample.

The length of school life varied from under a year to ten years. 3% of the sample were at school for a year or less; 2.4% for 2 years; 5% for 3 years; 17% for 4; 12.2% for 5; 9.7% for 6; 12.2% for 7; 19.5% for 8; 7.3% for 9 and 7.3% for 10 years.

The general pattern of progress through the school was for two or three years to be spent as 'readers' before moving into the 'writers' class. Richard Gowers, for example joined the school as a 'reader' in 1841 aged four years, spent three years in that class and then moved into the 'writers' for a further four years. Some children remained as 'readers' for their entire school life. George Maxim, for example started school aged four in 1838 and when he left in 1846 appears never to have moved into the 'writers' class. Others could obviously read before starting school, Charles Kimmis aged five in 1849 spent his entire school life in the 'writers' class until he left in 1846.

The 1833 Education Enquiry (8) shows that Hartest had two day schools; the Sparke's Charity with 73 free and fee-paying pupils; and a school opened in 1829 supported by voluntary contributions and fees, with 31 pupils. The Sunday School still continued to be supported by the parish at £4 a year and had 23 pupils. A private Boarding and Day school with 16 pupils had been opened in 1833.

Harriett Britten was the Governess and the school had twelve boarders aged between five and nine years. By 1844 Miss Ellen Death, then aged 21, had taken over the school, which in 1851 had seven boarders aged between eight and twelve years, from Suffolk, Essex and London. Some time between 1855 and 1861 Miss Jane Gill became the owner, and in the latter year it had sixteen boarders aged between five and fourteen years, from Suffolk, Norfolk, Essex and London. In 1871 she had only seven boarders aged between nine and fourteen from Suffolk and Essex. At the time of the Census in 1881 there were only two boarders aged 11 and 16 years, and by 1885 the school had closed.

In 1840 Sparke's Charity School became a member of the National Society, a Church of England organisation for aiding the education of the poor. In the same year the school had 57 pupils, 25 of which were paid for by the charity.

The Census Returns 1851-1881 were analysed to discover how many children there were in Hartest of a notional school age of five to fourteen years. These were divided into three categories, those who were scholars, those who had no occupation and were probably 'at home' and those out at work.

The results showed a very high proportion of children attending the National School long before education was compulsory, and that those 'at home' were always greater in number than those at work. In 1851, 54% of the children aged five to fourteen were scholars, 27.8% were at home and 18%

whose ages were between eight and fourteen were at work. In 1861, 56% were scholars, 29% at home and 14.4%, aged between nine and fourteen were at work. In 1871, 63.7% were scholars, 26.4% at home and 10.3%, aged between ten and fourteen were at work. In 1881, by which time children's attendance at school had been made compulsory throughout the country, 83% were scholars, only 2.7% at home and 14.2%, aged between eleven and fourteen at work.

No information has survived to indicate the position of the building used for the Free and later the National school. However, in 1859 a new site on the Boxted road was given by John George Weller Poley and a school built at a cost of £250. The money was raised partly by voluntary contributions and partly from the accumulated capital of Sparke's Charity. The school was enlarged in 1875 and the accommodation increased to hold 165 children. The same year the annual payments from the Charity were made as a contribution of £36 towards the salary of the schoolmaster.

In May 1879 the school at Boxted, built and financed by Mrs Weller Poley in 1852 closed and the children transferred to Hartest. The building at Hartest continued to be used as the village Church school until the present school was opened in 1966.

Head Teachers of Hartest School

No information exists before 1740.

Luke Boreham	1740–1779
John Crisp	1779–1810
Samuel Crisp	1810–1855
Sarah Smith	1855–1857
Mrs Hannah Maxim	1857–1863
Frederick Vickers	1863–1871
George Vickers	1871–1895
Mr Stanton	1896
Sheritt A. Long	1897–1924

Extracts from Hartest School Log Book (1)

Although our intention has been to study only the 19th century, we have taken a sample year every ten years from 1874–1924 in the hope that the latter years will remind our readers, especially those taught by Sheriff Long, of their schooldays.

1874

Jan	5	Cautioned boys about their remaining outside too long after the whistle has sounded.
	23	Punished AB who is a very bad boy.
	26	The Rector visits the School. Good progress. 1st and 2nd Classes wrote Dictation on paper.
	27	Third Standard Boys did maps of Suffolk (some on paper).
	29	1st Class wrote alphabet in the printing style. This tends to improve their writing and gives them a better idea of symetry etc.
Feb	3	Punished AB for ill behaviour.
	9	Several boys late in afternoon 'did not hear the whistle', ought to be a bell on school.
	11	Punished CD who is generally a good boy.
	12	Kept AB on till 1 o'clock, he having played truant previous day.
	18	First Class did maps of Europe on Slate.
	19	Several children 'dropping' in the fields.
	24	E, F & G kept in after school for being too talkative. Had a spelling lesson. Added singing to Time Table.
	25	Several 1st Class children absent. At work in the fields.
	26	HI who payed truant yesterday kept in one hour and stood in corner.
Mar	3	JK punished for talking while the Registers were being marked.
	10	Full school, weather being rough there is no field work for children.
	13	School inspected and examined by H.M. Inspector of Schools Mr W. Kefford.
	20	Drew out a New Time Table and submitted it to the Inspector. Restricted Needlework to 3 afternoons a week, instead of every afternoon.
	27	Taught a new song. Attendance falls off a little, weather being fine they have field work.

Apr 10 Commenced to teach 1st Class girls English Grammar by parsing a simple sentence. Boys had done it for a long time.

13 Received the Inspector's Report which is as follows:

'The result of the Examination is unsatisfactory. Reading is hurried. Writing and Spelling defective, and Arithmetic almost nil. The Managers ought at once to improve the internal arrangements of the school: under the present circumstances it is impossible for the master to impart instruction or maintain good discipline. Convenient parallel desks must be supplied. Among the other requirements are black boards and easels, suitable desk for the master, additional Reading Books, Admission Register school portfolio, supply of sewing materials for girls.

The defects in the school furniture and apparatus must be made good without delay.'

24 Many children away on account of 'The Fair'. Cautioned them about it.

May 1 First Class children fall off in their attendance, many at field work.

8 Taught children a New Song 'Resolution'.

15 LM left school to go as errand boy.

22 Whitsuntide vacation commences.

Jun 1 School reopens, with good attendance.

9 New desks and apparatus provided for the school.

19 By help of new desks etc. better discipline maintained and instruction more effectually imparted.

26 Attendance of children fall short; much work in fields and haymeadows.

Jul 24 Find the Second Class Children's Arithmetic much improved. Attendance low, the Harvest operations having commenced.

31 Attendance lower than last week.

Aug 7 Harvest vacation commences.

Sept 7 School reopens with small attendance there being still field work.

14 Punished NO for repeated acts of idleness and insubordination to monitor.

Oct 5 A large attendance of little ones makes very hard work.

12 Feel want of more teaching power.

19 Cautioned several boys about coming to school with dirty hands.

Dec 14 Very low attendance especially of girls the weather being very inclement.

24 Christmas Vacation commences.

1884

Jan 7 School re-opens with fair attendance.

14 Rector heard 1st Class Reading Lesson in Geographical Readers.

21 New Books procured viz 6 Standard III, 1½ dozen Standard I, 1 dozen Standard II Reading Books. ¼ Ream of Paper.

Feb 8 H.M. Inspector's annual visit.
List of Songs:– Canadian Boat Song, Two Rounds (sung), The Blacksmith, The Months, Resolution, The Violet, The Laughing Rill (sung) and Merry Xmas.

12 Received Schedule of Passes from HM Inspector. Passes as follows Reading 42, Writing 33, Arithmetic 30.

26 Gave ½ holiday on Shrove-Tuesday.

Mar 3 5 doz. new copy Books, and quart bottle of Ink.

5 Her Majesty's Inspector's Report on Examinations received for 1884. The boys have passed a pretty fair Examination, but there are weak points about their work. The first Standard is weak in all Subjects. Arithmetic in the fifth Standard is faulty and Notation needs attention in the Second Standard. The Repetition was fairly well said and the Grammar exercise was fairly done. Only moderate progress has been made in Geography. The Boys were inclined to talk during the Examination.

12 Bills for Schooling of Children from Boxted and Somerton.
Boxted 17 at 18s. 6d. = £24 19s. 6d.; Somerton 18 at 18s. 6d. = £16 13s. 0d. Total £41 12s. 6d.

Apr 7 Rector gave permission for Easter Holiday to commence on 10th at noon.

21 School re-assembled after a weeks vacation. New Cupboard for Books, Slates etc.

May 5 Standard V began Simple Proportion.

19 New Map of Holy Land for Scripture Teaching.

26 Rector consented to give 1 weeks holiday to the School commencing on Thursday 29th at 4.0 pm.

Jun 11 Diocesan Inspection this morning. Rev A. S. Stokes.

23 Received a Report of Diocesan Inspector. School reported 'Fair'.

Jul 21 Rector examined Copy Book Writing in Upper Standards.

28 Scholars had holiday. Choir trip to Harwich via Ipswich.

29 Attendance Officer (Mr A. Chaplin) visited the School in Morning.

Aug	8	Harvest vacation commences today at 12. 5 weeks.
Sept	15	School re-opens with very fair attendance.
Nov	18	Standard I, all the boys in this Standard present this morning (remarkable).
Dec	16	Rector gave permission for Xmas holidays to commence on Friday 19th at noon (2 weeks).

1894

Jan	2	School reopens after 1 weeks holiday.
	16	Drawing Examination conducted by Capt H. Woolner, commenced at 1 pm.
	31	Average attendance for year 38. School songs 1894:– Boat Song, Roses, Murmer Gentle Lyre, When there's love at Home, The Smith.
Feb	5	School Inspected. H. W. Claughton.
	9	Admitted several little boys from Infants Department.
Mar	1	Rev A. Packer brought in the Report of H.M. Inspector. 'Some progress has been made in the lower Standards but Arithmetic is very weak in the 4th and 5th Standards. The Grant for English is barely earned. There is no cloakroom accommodation for the Boys.'
	22	School closes for Easter holidays of 1 week.
Apr	2	School reopens—attendance small.
	10	Rector came in, required a list of Boys who had attended above 410 times during the last school year. These were Ernest Sturgeon (425) aged 10 in Standard 4, and George Quantrill (416) aged 8 in Standard 2.
	20	Average attendance for week 38.4, on Books 46.
	27	Poetry for next Examination:– Standard 1, Two Crossing Sweepers; Standard 2. The Little Orphan; Standard 3. The Blacksmith; Standard 4. After Blenheim; Standards 5, 6 and 7, Lay of the Last Minstrel.
May	11	Broke up for Whitsun holidays (1 week).
Jun	15	School Attendance Officers brought New Copy of 'Bye-laws' for Sudbury Union School Attendance Committee.

Jul 3 Scripture examination in morning by Rev A. S. Stokes. Half holiday in the afternoon.

10 Report of Diocesan Inspector is as under:– The written work was Good and the memory work was Good on the whole although somewhat wanting in accuracy. Answering uneven. School reported 'Very Fair'.

20 Average attendance 34.1. Several ill, others haying.

27 Average attendance falls to 30.9. Continued illness among boys. All Somerton boys absent. Average attendance for Quarter ending July 27 — 35.

Aug 10 Received Circular letter 146, from Science and Arts Department relating to Drawing in Standard I and II.

12 School closed for Harvest Holidays.

Sep 16 School re-opened after 5 weeks holidays.

Nov 5 Rev A. Packer visitor. The usual ½ holiday given by permission.

8 1 dozen new slates for Standard II, 1 box of steel pens procured for school.

15 3 dozen Ivy Copy Books provided.

Dec 21 School breaks up for Xmas holidays.

31 School re-assembles after 1 weeks holiday.

1904

Jan 18 Attendance Officer visited today.

29 The Headmaster was absent from School Thursday Jan 28th and Wednesday Afternoon Jan 27th by permission.

Feb 4 There are 58 claimants for the quarterly certificate of Attendance. I have today sent the list to the Secretary.

16 Usual Half holiday (Shrove Tuesday).

29 Lessons for the School year 1904.

Geography: Standards 1–3 'England'; Standards 4–6 'Europe'
History: Standards 4-6 'Life of Queen Victoria'
Object Lessons: Standard 1–3 Common Objects; Standards 4–6 Elementary Science
Drawing — Boys
Sewing — Girls
Singing — Boys and Girls
Repetition. Standard 1 and 2: 'The Dog at his Masters Grave'
Standard 3 'Bruce and the Spider'
Standard 4–6 'Edinburgh after Flodden'

Mar 8 Sickness greatly affects the attendance. The sickness is chiefly among juniors.

11 Four scholars went to Shimpling to be examined by H.M.I. for Total Exemption Certificates. Mabel Bradnam and Arthur Willoughby passed.

21 Master absent until 9.45 am to go to Boxted Hall to see Squire Poley.

22 Report: Mixed School; The attendance is satisfactory and the general progress is creditable. Drill should be taken by sections, as the available space is very small.

Infants Class, The Infants Class continues to make fairly good Progress.

25 A Holiday given today (afternoon) by permission of the Manager through the Rector, to enable candidates to attend the confirmation service at Long Melford.

Apr 8 The usual half holiday given today following an Inspection of the School.

May 13 A Half Holiday given today by order of the Correspondent to enable the School to be got ready for a concert in the evening. Percentage of Attendance for week 98%.

18 The children were allowed to go on the green at 10.15 am to witness the movements of the Essex Yeomanry. They (children) returned to school at 11 am.

20 School closed for Whit week.

Jul 4 Mr E. B. King commenced duties this morning.

7 Drill taken with boys instead of Drawing as yesterdays drill was prevented by rain.

18 School Examined in Scripture today by the Rev Banks Williams.

22 Philip Clarke (13) and William Sturgeon (13) have been granted certificates today for total exemption being above the age of 13 years and having satisfied the requirements as to attendance for 5 years.

Aug 2 A holiday yesterday (Monday) it being Bank Holiday.

10 Closed School for Harvest Holidays (5 weeks).

Sep 21 Two cases of whooping cough affect the attendance to a small degree.

Oct 21 The usual ½ holiday given today following the Inspection by H.M.I.

Nov 10 Started coming in School in the afternoon at 1 instead of 2 pm.
28 Received copy of H.M.I.s Report which is as follows:–
Mixed—The staff was increased in July, and the School is now doing very well. Another cupboard is much wanted.

1914

Jan 12 Reopened School after Xmas Holidays. 103 out of 111 attended.

Feb 16 Whooping Cough and Chicken Pox very bad attendance 71.
25 Ash Wednesday. The children did not go to Church as specified on Time Table. The fact of the Whooping Cough infection among scholars and the great number of colds, it was thought that children would be better off in school.

Mar 4 Inspection 26th January 1914. Report by HMI Mr F. W. Thompson. Since the last report the offices have been reconstructed and the lighting in the main room has been much improved, and is now satisfactory. No partition has yet been erected though there are as a rule three teachers at work in the room. More room is needed for the girls' and Infants cloaks which were hanging one above another in three rows on the day of the visit of inspection. A fixture for handbasins is required. There is no guard for the stove in the main room. Many of the desks have much too great a 'horizontal distance' between the edge of the desk and the seat.
12 Registers not marked today. A very wet and stormy day. Attendance 34. Morning spent in drying clothes.
13 Log Book sent to Boxted Hall today for Managers meeting.
22 No gardening on March 2, 6, 9, 13, 16, 20 on account of bad weather.

Apr 9 Closed for Easter Holiday.
20 Reopened after Easter Holidays.

May 6 Mrs Long and Miss Hibble absent from 9.15 to 9.30 to see doctor.
18 Mr Creek visited pm and took gardening lesson.

Scheme for 1914

Class I

Geography	South Africa
History	Lives of Great Men
Arithmetic	Theoretical, practical, problematical application to usual rules for Standard 4–6; Practical instruction in Mensuration Decimal system, weights and measures.

English	Composition, Letter Writing, Word Work etc.
Hygiene	Physical Training, Breathing, Food etc.
Nature Study	Gardening for boys. Lessons on plants, insects etc.
Recitation	'Charge of the Light Brigade' etc.

Class 2

Geography	England with special knowledge of Suffolk
History	Lives of Noted persons
Arithmetic	Money, Weights and Measures. Practical and Problematical.
English	Sentence forming, Composition and letter writing.
Hygiene	Physical Training, Food, Cleanliness etc.
Nature Study	Plants, Flowers etc.
Recitation	'Nelly's Shilling' etc.

Class 3

Geography	Own neighbourhood, directions and general information.
History	Stories from English History
Arithmetic	Simple rules and problems
English	Word building, Sentence forming, oral and written.
Hygiene	Physical Training, Cleanliness etc.
Nature Study	Plants, Animals etc.
Recitation	'The Wood Mouse' etc.

28 Broke up for Whitsuntide holidays (1 week)

Jun 17 Dr Hopkins visited for Medical Examination of Children
25 School opened for 1.30 instead of 2.00 to allow Boxted Children to attend a treat.

Jul 8 Holiday in afternoon, on account of School Treat
9 Register not marked today on account of Diocesan Inspection.
14 Dr Bygott visited today and dealt with three cases of verminous heads.
16 School closed today to enable children to go to seaside (Clacton).
23 School closed today for Chadacre Flower Show

Aug 3 Bank Holiday—holiday
7 Closed for Harvest Holidays. 5 weeks.

Sep 22 Master absent today pm to attend the funeral of Mr Robert Aldredge (late manager) who died 16th September.

Oct	20	Mr Creek, Horticultural Instructor visited yesterday.
Nov	23	Mr Creek visited, planted apple trees etc.
Dec	10	Registers not marked today. A very wet day. 1.46 inches of rain in 24 hours ending 9 am.
	23	School closed for Xmas Holidays to reopen 11 Jan 1915.

1924

Jan	7	Reopened school after Xmas Holidays.
	21	Four cases of measles reported today to Medical Officer.
Feb	11	School closed through Measles.
Mar	24	Reopened school after 6 weeks closure through Measles.
Apr	11	A very heavy snow storm. Register not marked, Attendance only 32 out of 97 in morning, and 33 in the afternoon.
	28	Reopened School after Easter Holidays.
	30	I have today given up charge of this school as Headteacher after a period of 27⅓ years. Mrs Long also leaves today. Sheriff A. Long.
May	1	Taking charge pending the arrival of a fresh Headteacher H. Oliver Punchard.
	2	Miss M. H. Russel commenced duties as Assistant Teacher. Medical Inspection by Dr Cross YZ sent home under instruction of School Medical Officer because of verminous state of her head.
	19	I have today taken charge of this school as Head Mistress Edith Aves.
	20	Mrs Poley (Manager) visited today about collection for Alexandra Rose Day Fund.
	29	Ascension Day. Attended service at Church at 11 am.
Jun	11	School reopened after Whitsun holidays (two days).
	19	Miss Brown, county instructress in Needlework inspected work.
	25	Received letter from Mr Creek respecting damage done by sheep on allotment when boys gardening on Monday last.
Jul	7	School closed for days holiday owing to Sunday School treat for village children
Aug	14	Assistant Medical Officer visited today, to test two childrens eyes.
	15	School closed till September 22nd for Summer holiday.

Oct	1	Rev Finch (of Stanstead) Diocesan Inspector visited. Winter Session commenced—School closing at 3.40 pm.
Nov	11	Armistice Day. Two minutes silence observed in school after which wreath placed on War Memorial by children.
	25	Dr D. M. McCullagh, Dental Surgeon, visited today 1.30 pm and examined teeth of children of seven years and under.
Dec	12	School Concert in Institute at 7 pm to raise funds for purchase of a School Piano. £10 realised.
	18	School closed for Christmas holidays until 5th January.

Sheriff Augustus Long: schoolmaster of Hartest 1897–1924.

Miss Caroline Gibbons and her class, c.1906: she taught at the school from about 1888–1907.

Back Row: left to right; Walter Reynolds of Dowsetts; Fred Bird of Boxted; Honour Simpson of Boxted; ?; Wilfred Eley of Waldgraves; Mary Stewart of Chadacre; Violet Honeyball who lived behind Ince's barn at the Duddery; ?; Edith Pain Hartest Hill; Frank Johnson of Round House.

Middle Row: Edith Sturgeon the Green; Alred Cadge; Sidney Payne Hartest Hill; ?; ? Pettitt; ? Pettitt; Ernie Willoughby of Round House Cottage; ?; Walter —— of Potash.

Front Row: Lila Procter; ?; ?; Hilda Johnson of the Mill; ?; Ivy Pask of Place Farm; —— Payne; Winnie Sturgeon of 'Sturgeons' now 'Vintens'; Walter Hines of Mill Hill Farm.

Postal Services

In October 1825 five inhabitants of Bradfield St Clare, Cockfield and Lavenham sent a petition to Francis Freeling, Secretary to the Post Master General in London. They complained about the delay in receiving their mail via Sudbury and Long Melford, and suggested that a route could be established directly from Bury St Edmunds.

The local Surveyor to the General Post Office, Mr Graham Hart, was asked to investigate the situation. He proposed that a route or 'walk' be introduced as a Penny Post between Bury and Lavenham via Hartest. The route was to be from Bury to Hawstead then to Lawshall and end at Hartest. Robert Gill, already employed as a '. . . private Messenger who now conveys the letters from Bury as far as the Village of Hartest . . .' (1) was to become the official Messenger, at a salary of 14s. a week. He was to wait at Hartest while another messenger took the mail to Lavenham and returned with the bag for Bury. The cost was expected to be £54 12s. a year, and the income from the penny post was estimated at £40. The Earl of Chichester, Post Master General, agreed to the arrangements for an experimental period of twelve months.

In January 1827 Robert Gill applied for an increase in wages from 14s. to 17s. 6d. a week because, as he wrote '. . . since the Alterations have taken place with respect to the Post Office I can positively declare and that with truth that I have upon an Average been losing 4 shillings per week . . .' (2). Francis Freeling recommended, and the Post Master General agreed, that Gill's wages should be raised to 16s. a week.

During the experimental twelve months the route had processed about 4,680 Penny Post letters and about 7,750 general and 'bye' letters. Freeling recommended that the route should become permanent and it continued to be serviced by foot messengers until 1879.

In 1831, in response to a petition from the inhabitants of Long Melford, the second stage of the route was diverted to reach Lavenham via Melford. The mail now left Bury at 7 am, reached Hartest at 9 am, where it was handed over to the second Messenger who walked to Melford by 11.30, collected the Sudbury mail and proceeded to Lavenham by 12.30, then returning directly to Hartest.

Mr Thomas Halifax of Chadacre Hall was asked, by Sir Francis Freeling, to express an opinion on the new plan. Although it meant that he would have to send to Hartest for his mail each morning he would '. . . be quite contented to do so, if the plan is found to be generally beneficial, which I trust it will, provided the hours named are punctually adhered to, especially at Bury and Sudbury . . .' (3).

The Post Office staff records have been lost prior to 1844. However, a Receiver of Mail had been appointed at Hartest before then, as he resigned in December 1844. In February 1845 John Kimmis was appointed Receiver at a salary of £4 a year. He was described as a shoemaker aged 54 in the 1851

Census and lived on the Green. In 1838 he was Parish Clerk receiving £6 a year, and in that year was declared an insolvent debtor.

Elizabeth Kimmis, widow of John, was postmistress in the 1861 Census. Their son George also a shoemaker and Parish Clerk, became postmaster between 1871 and 1874 and continued until about 1904 when his widow Louisa was the postmistress. The footmessenger was eventually replaced by a mail cart delivery in June 1879. The 1884 Ordnance Survey map shows the Post Office to have been next to the Smithy at the foot of Hartest Hill.

Until c.1880 mail was delivered and collected once a day, when the messenger arrived from Bury at 9 am. and returned at 5 pm. The 1885 Directory records that the Post Office now included a Money Order Office and a Savings Bank by 1888, and that mail arrived at 6.30 am. and was collected at 6 pm. except on Sunday when it was collected at 12.30 pm.

In 1906 George Redgrave, grandson of George Kimmis, became Postmaster. By 1908 a twice daily mail service had been introduced, deliveries being made at 6.30 am. and 3.40 pm. and collections at 10.30 am. and 6 pm, except on Sundays when it arrived at 6.45 am and was collected at 12.20 pm. Mr Redgrave remained as Postmaster until 1951, when he was succeeded by his daughter Miss Ethel Redgrave, who retired in 1967. While the Redgrave family were Postmasters the office was based at the house anciently known as 'Hunters' or the 'Bricked House'.

Mrs Peggy Harling took over as Postmistress in 1967 and the business moved to its present site.

The Post Office, ?c.1916: the dating of this photograph has proved difficult. The house called 'Hunters' became the Post Office in 1906; the poster displays 'His Majesties Foot Guards'; and there are lady letter deliverers. All this evidence points to the First World War when women would have been employed.

Left to right: Miss Redgrave (in doorway); Abraham Ling (on mail-cart); ?; Alfred Cadge; Lil Hibble; Jessie Parton; Edmund Dye; ?; ?.

The Bell Inn, ?c.1916: this photograph seems to have been taken the same day as that outside the Post Office. George Stiff was the tenant from c.1906–c.1920. F. C. Christmas & Co brewers of Haverhill were the owners of the Bell.

Melford Rural District Road Crew, ?c.1913: the Minutes of the Melford R.D.C. 'Main Roads Committee' record that the roads in Hartest were rolled with granite and pit-stone in early 1913. The steam rollers were hired from The Edison Steam Rolling Company and Messers Doran Brothers.

Left to right: ?; ?; George Garwood, Ernest Dye.

Queen Victoria's Jubilee Celebrations

The 'Bury and Norwich Post' reported the celebrations at Boxted and Hartest for the Queen's Golden Jubilee in 1887 as follows:–

'HARTEST-CUM-BOXTED. — The Jubilee celebration commenced here at an early hour on Tuesday morning. Just after 4 o'clock the church bells rang out merry peals, followed at intervals by firing of cannons. Flags floated from the cottage windows, from the trees, and from the church tower. At noon service was held in the church, which was well attended. The esteemed rector, the Rev A. Packer, preached an eloquent sermon from the lesson for the Jubilee thanksgiving, "Fear God: Honour the King." The members of the Foresters', Shepherds' and Oddfellows' Friendly Societies established in the village attended in their regalia.

'At the close of the service the rector planted a tree in the churchyard in commemoration of the Jubilee, after which the company marched to the strains of the Hartest Drum and Fife Band to Boxted Hall Park kindly lent for the occasion by worthy Squire J. G. Weller Poley, whose gardens were thrown open to the people at 4 o'clock. About 250 men sat down in a large tent erected in front of the Hall to a capital dinner which had been cooked in the Squire's kitchen. "The health of the Queen" was proposed by the rector in eulogistic terms, the Rev. gentleman quoting statistics, showing the progress of the nation during the Victorian era. At half-past four the women and children numbering about 520 were regaled with a capital meat tea. A variety of sports were engaged in during the afternoon and some clever conjuring tricks were performed by a gentleman amateur to the great astonishment of the beholders. The proceedings closed with a display of fireworks, after which hearty cheers were given for Mr. Poley for the use of the grounds, and for the members of the Committee for the pains taken to provide for the enjoyment of the parishioners of both parishes.' (1)

Ten years later the Diamond Jubilee celebrations were organised by Mr George King, of Townsend Farm, and Mr Sheriff Long the schoolmaster. The events were reported as follows:–

'HARTEST — on Tuesday last, the Jubilee of the Queen's reign for 60 years, there was great rejoicing in this parish. The church bells began to ring at five in the morning, and continued at intervals throughout the day. Flags and bannerets were suspended from the Club, shops and cottages around the village green. At three o'clock, 230 labourers and tradesmen were bountifully provided with a dinner of roast beef and plum pudding, and three glasses of "Greene's AK." in Mr King's malting. At four o'clock, about 160 children had tea, cake, bread-and-butter, and roast beef, in Mr King's barn, near the malting, and at five o'clock, over 300 mothers and their children had a similar tea in Mr King's malting, and lastly, the Rector and the Rev J. A. Davenport, Mr Mrs and Miss Bent, the farmers, together with their wives and children, shop-keepers, and others had their tea together. About 700 were provided with dinner and tea. We understand that 530 lbs of beef was provided, and about 150 lbs of plum-pudding most of which was cooked at Mr King's house, and all the tea for over 500 children and their mothers, was made there, under the direction of Mrs King. Too much praise cannot be given to Mr and Mrs King for the admirable way with which everything was planned and carried out.

'In the field adjoining, kindly lent by Mr George Abbott, of Brick House Farm, all the guests resorted, and spent a very pleasant evening in sports, racing for prizes, swings suspended from large oak trees, scrambling for a bushel of nuts, sweets and biscuits, etc. At nine o'clock a sandwich was given to each, and all the labourers were provided with beer during the evening. At ten o'clock there was a splendid exhibition of fireworks, purchased at the Crystal Palace, and some were made by Mr Sheriff Long, schoolmaster; who most successfully made all the arrangements for the exhibition, which came to an end at about eleven o'clock. After dinner the Rector proposed "The health of the Queen," and spoke of her long and successful reign, and of the blessings we all enjoyed as Englishmen—how our colonies had increased in her reign, so that one-fifth of the whole land of the world, and more than one-fifth of all its inhabitants, were governed by our Queen of England and Empress of India. A medal was given by the Rector to each of the Sunday School scholars, and to some others in the parish. Mr Thomas Weller Poley of West Burgh, Chichester, brother of the Squire, has recently given to the parish a very handsome set of twelve new hand bells, and they were rung for the first time on Jubilee day, during the festivities in the evening.' (2)

Foresters' Procession in the Row, c.1914: notice the 'The Row' on the left.

Hartest Fair

The Fair was held annually on St George's Day, and the day following, from 1789 until the late 1950s. Its origin was a national thanksgiving, held on 23 April 1789, for the recovery of King George III 'from an afflictive malady' (madness). At Hartest on that day the inhabitants '. . . to evince their loyalty congregated at the stone to drink and make merry and from this very circumstance originated the wake or fair' (1).

Between 1814 and 1826 it was described as being for the sale of cattle and toys, from which we may infer it was mainly a pleasure fair. It obviously had little trading significance, as it is not mentioned in any of the 19th century county directories.

In the 1841 census, the row of cottages that stood between the corner of 'The Forge' and the bridge, were called the 'Duddery'. This name still exists, and indicates a place where clothes were sold. It is almost certain that this activity was associated with the fair.

Within living memory, Hartest fair was a time for local rivalries to be settled between the boys of the surrounding villages. The 'Bury and Norwich Post' on 30 April 1845 reported an affray as follows:–

'A serious breach of the peace was committed at Hartest Fair on Wednesday night last (23 April). At twelve o'clock the police in execution of their orders, cleared the public houses and drinking booths, but a number of persons congregated on the green, and soon after commenced an assault upon the officers when one man (David Mason, labourer aged 20) was arrested in the act of striking a constable (John Burroughs), upon which a general attack was made upon them, in which the sergeant of police (John Wade) was severely cut by a blow from a stone, his staff wrested from him (by William Pettit, labourer, aged 48), and the prisoner rescued. The sergeant was so stunned by the blow and loss of blood, that it was necessary to carry him into the house of Mr King, the surgeon, by whom his wounds were dressed. On the following day Major Griffith ordered a sufficient force to attend to prevent any repetition of the disorders, and was himself present for several hours, the effect of which was that at twelve o'clock that night every place was quietly and peaceably cleared. On Friday two men, named David Mason and William Pettit were convicted at the Melford Petty Sessions of assaulting the police, and sentenced to pay the former £2 7s. 6d. and the latter £5, or be imprisoned two calendar months.'

Hartest Fair, c.1910: the waggon the right is inscribed, 'Patronised by the Nobility', and the name 'Creighton' can be made out behind the swinging-boats.

The Green, c.1903: notice the two girls with a bassinet or baby-carriage, the blacksmiths shop, and the saw-pit in the background. On the back of the photograph is written '. . . the bigstone is what old Stephen Baynton used to jump over after walking to Bury and Back!

Hartest Stone

The earliest documentary evidence about the stone comes from the 'Bury and Norwich Post' newspaper of July 1859. The Suffolk Institute of Archaeology visited Hartest in June, the members examined the stone and the suggestion made that '. . . its site (was) probably one of the ancient tut-hills' (1).

In July, Charles Mills, Master of a day and boarding school in Somerton wrote two letters to the newspaper explaining why the stone was on Hartest Green (2).

It appears the stone was dug out of High Field in Somerton which then formed part of Mile End Farm, Hartest. In 1712 Mr Marks of Rivets Hall suggested that it be moved to the Green to commemorate the victories of the Duke of Marlborough in the war of the Spanish Succession. The end of the war was marked by the treaty of Utrecht, signed on 11 April 1713 and a day of national thanksgiving on 7 July. Either of these two events might have been the focus of the activity in Hartest. A sledge was constructed and the stone, with Mr Marks on top, blowing a trumpet, was pulled to Hartest Green by 45 horses. After positioning the stone the rest of the day was spent in feasting and rejoicing.

The stone continued to be the centre of village celebrations throughout the 18th century, the inhabitants using it as 'a table for their drink'.

Other similar, although smaller, stones are to be found locally at Lidgate Castle and the Plumbers Arms at Denston. These stones are called 'Glacial Erratics' because they were brought by glaciers from other geological areas of the country during the Ice Age, and deposited as the ice eventually melted.

Such stones are still ploughed up in the parish, the most recent being in 1983 from Mill Field on the Somerton road.

Alexandra Rose Day, 1920.

Hospital Sunday, 1920.

Letters from the Rev. Arthur Packer to John Weller Poley

The Rev. Arthur Packer was Rector of Hartest and Boxted from 1878 to 1905. He was also a trustee of the charity established by John Poley in 1572. Each year in December, between 1887 and 1895, he wrote to Squire John George Weller Poley thanking him for the charity money. He also commented on local events and the administration of the charity. Unfortunately the Squire only kept the part of the letter that served as the receipt for the money, and so at least half of each letter is missing. The following extracts give the flavour of Hartest life as seen by a concerned clergyman (1).

28 December 1888. 'The Church Wardens of Hartest begin to distribute the coals last Saturday and will continue to do so every Saturday as long as the money and subscriptions last. I will make it known on Sunday to the Boxted people when their money is to be given away.'

10 December 1889. 'I am glad you are going to have the ground levelled in front of the Club, and when it is planted with shrubs it will be an ornament to the green and a lasting monument to your liberality. Your proposal to visit the Club in the spring before it closes is a very good one. I never entered the Club in the evening the whole of last session, but left it to the entire management of the Committee, but was often told of the bad behaviour of the young members and their annoyance to the older ones.' (rest lost)

1890. 'It was with difficulty I reached home last night, the snow in the roads was so deep and it was bitterly cold. The poor labourers will be unable to work in the fields and the loss of a day or twos work in a week makes it very trying for those who have families.'

15 January 1892. 'We commenced giving away coals weekly the day before Christmas day, and Mr. King very kindly carts the coals free of charge which saves us 3s. a ton.

'Hartest is suffering dreadfully from influenza. I think there are nearly 40 ill of it and our School Mistress (Miss Alice Young) have been ill for a fortnight and unable to attend school, which is most unfortunate because the annual examination by Government Inspector takes place on February 5. I hope you and Mrs. Poley have escaped and will escape this influenza which I believe to be very infectious if not contagious.

'The cold has been most intense and very trying for the poor who are poorly clad and have cold miserable cottages.

'Wishing you a happy new year, with kind regards to Mrs. Poley. Believe me to be yours Sincerely Arthur Packer.'

2 January 1893. 'Last Friday the woods at Chadacre were shot through, and I hear the seven guns killed 40 pheasants but there was shooting enough to have killed 400. I never heard anything like it. The French might have landed the firing was incessant . . .'

In 1894 Parish Council were established and could assume responsibility for secular charities.

In the next extract Rev. Packer describes the difficulties of distributing the coal and is very pleased to hand over the responsibility to the Council.

December 1894. 'This I have done for 15 years . . . The list of recipients of the coals is kept in the coal house and is seen by all who have coals, and each one knows how much the others have. If anyone by mistake gets a peck to much I am quickly informed of it. Sometimes a Child have been very recently been born and I was not aware of it. Also sometimes the Child has gone to work and therefore the parents are not entitled to Coals for that Child, but I was not aware the Child was working. But I am very soon made acquainted with it by their neighbours. I shall be very glad to hand over the part I take in the distribution of the Charity, for neither Mr. King (Churchwarden) nor I can please the recipients of the charity. It takes me a great deal of time and trouble and I receive no thanks but the contrary . . .'

The Green, c.1904: taken the same day as the other view of Crickmores shop and the Chapel. Seated on the stone is Mrs Kate Dye, standing next to her is her mother Mrs Susan Maxim, wife of John Maxim, bricklayer. If the photograph was taken in 1904, then Kate would have been 27 and Susan 60 years old.

Hartest and Boxted Institute

The building was paid for by Thomas Weller Poley, brother of the Lord of the Manor, designed by Reginald Blomfield, and built in 1888 by Thomas Cadge of Hartest. The 1891 Directory described it as '. . . one large hall about 45 feet by 25 feet, with Kitchen, offices and a caretakers room attached . . . it is well supplied with daily and other papers, a bagateel board etc. . . .'

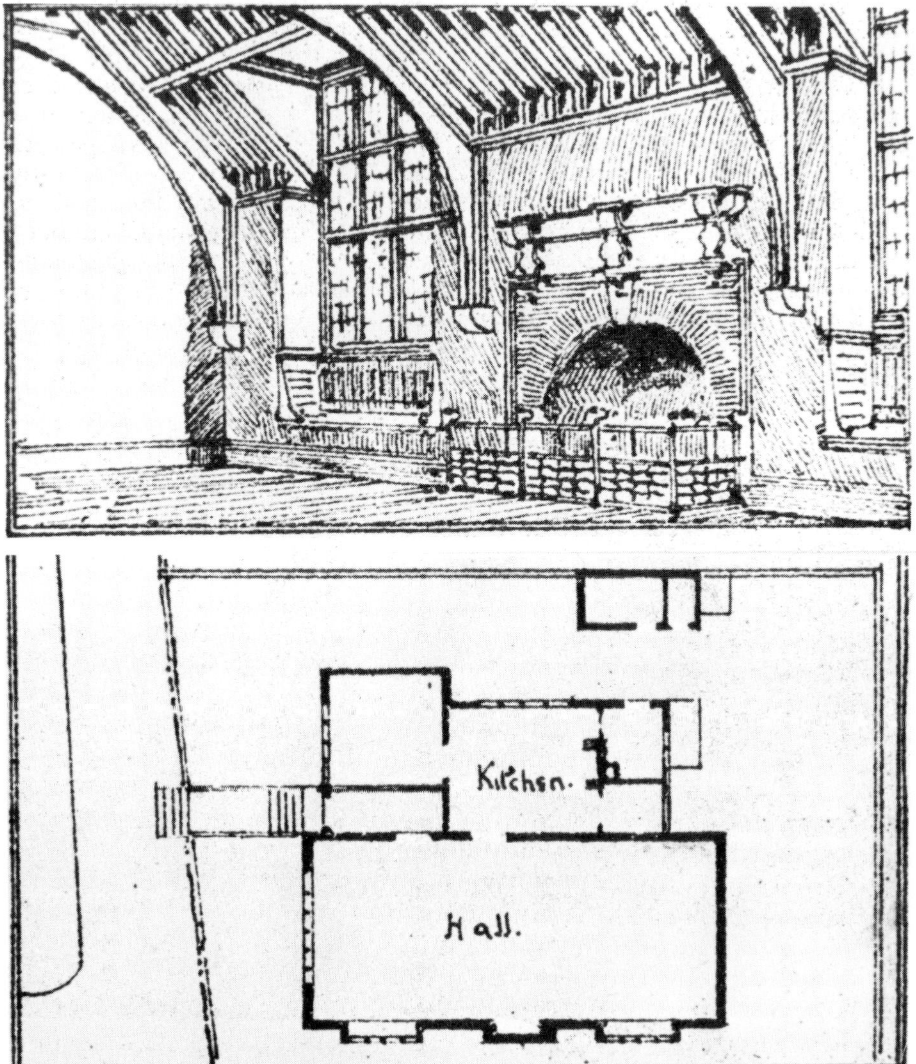

Interior view and plan of the Institute 1888.

Hartest in 1896

HARTEST is a parish and village 9 miles north-by-west from Sudbury, 6 north-west from Long Melford and 4½ north from Glemsford station on the Cambridge and Long Melford section of the Great Eastern railway, in the Southern division of the county, hundred of Babergh, Melford petty sessional division, union and county court district of Sudbury, rural deanery and archdeaconry of Sudbury and diocese of Ely. The church of All Saints is a structure of flint in the Perpendicular style, consisting of chancel, nave, aisles, north and south porches and an embattled western tower of flint and brick, containing 5 bells: the stained east window, a memorial to the late Mrs. Maddy, was erected by Miss Sawyer, niece of the late Rev. John Maddy D.D. rector here from 1819 and canon of Ely; there is another memorial window to John Dickerson, and a marble monument, erected 1891, in memory of the Rev. W. Weller-Poley M.A. rector of Santon 1857-86, by his widow, who also restored both porches, and the tower was also restored by her in 1890 as a memorial of her husband: the church was restored and reseated in 1879 at a cost of £1,200, and has 400 sittings. The register dates from the year 1556. The living is a rectory, consolidated with that of Boxted, average tithe rent-charge £720, net yearly value £500, including 20 acres of glebe and residence, in the gift of the Crown, and held since 1878 by the Rev. Arthur Packer M.A. of St. Edmund Hall, Oxford, rural dean of Sudbury, and J.P. for Suffolk. In the village is a small Congregational chapel and there is a meeting room for the Plymouth Brethren. The Village Institute, erected in 1888, by Thomas Weller-Poley esq. of London, has now (1896) about 100 members. A cemetery of half an acre was formed in 1857 at a cost of £196, and is under the control of the Parish Council. Two cottages, left by Thomas Wright in 1646, with an annual sum of 10s. were sold in 1869 for £18, which amount was invested and the interest is applied towards the relief of four poor widows. The poor of Hartest have also 20s. yearly from Corder's charity, and a fifth part of Poley's charity, amounting to £11 8s. yearly. John George Weller-Poley esq. of Boxted Hall, is lord of the manor and principal landowner. The soil is heavy loam; subsoil, chiefly clay. The chief crops are wheat, barley, oats, beans, peas and roots. The area is 1,964 acres of land; rateable value, £2,216; the population in 1891 was 590.

Parish Clerk, Charles Dye.

Post & M. O. O., S. B. & Annuity & Insurance Office.—George Kimmis, sub-postmaster. Letters arrive through Bury St. Edmunds at 6.30 a.m.; dispatched at 6 p.m. The nearest telegraph office is at Glemsford

Thomas Sparke, in 1721, bequeathed a house & land, now producing a yearly income of £30 (out of which £6 is paid to Brockley school & £1 to Hawkedon school), which is applied to the school

National School (mixed), built in 1860 & enlarged in 1875, for 180 children; average attendance, 150; Joseph Stanton, master; Mrs. Alice Stanton, mistress; Miss Caroline Gibbons, infants' mistress

Carriers to—

Bury—William Pask, mon. wed. & sat.; Alfred Dye, wed. & sat

Sudbury—Alfred Dye, thurs

PRIVATE RESIDENTS.

Bent Baldwin Harry, Stow hill
Cawston Mrs
Davenport Rev. James Arthur M.A. (curate)
Kendall William Thomas
Nicholls Lucius
Packer Rev. Arthur M.A., J.P. (& rural dean), Rectory

COMMERCIAL.

Aldridge Robert, baker & shoe maker
Bailey Moses, shopkeeper
Bradnam Jn. cattle dealer & farmer
Cadge Herbert, builder
Cawston William Ebenezer, farmer
Cawston Geo. Bateman, frmr. & btchr
Cemetery (Frederick Sturgeon, kpr)
Clarke Benjamin, butcher
Clarke Florence (Miss), shopkeeper
Colson Charles, farmer
Crickmore John, grocer & draper
Dye Alfred, beer retailer & carrier
Ellingham Clement, baker
Foreman Eliza (Mrs.), shopkeeper
Game Alfred, Bell inn
Gunn Joseph Hines, farmer, Walgrave's farm
Hayward James, carpenter
Honeywood James, farmer
Honeywood John, farmer
Hudgell William, harness maker
Kimmis Geo. shoe mkr. & post office
King Geo. farmer, maltster & miller (wind & steam)
Nicholls Lucius, surgeon, & medical officer & public vaccinator No. 1 district, Sudbury union & No. 8 district, Thingoe union
Pask Frederick, baker
Pask William, carrier & shopkeeper
Pawsey Charles, Swan P.H
Savage Charles, Cook's farm
Spilling Daniel, harness maker
Sturgeon Edwd. organ buildr.& baker
Sturgeon Robt. plumber & decorator
Tabner George, Crown inn
Village Institute (Wm. Mills, sec)

Taken from The Directory of Suffolk, by Kelly & Co. 1892.

Notes

Abbreviations

HLRO	House of Lords Record Office.
NRO	Norfolk Record Office.
POA	Post Office Archives.
PRO	Public Record Office.
SIA	*Suffolk Institute of Archaeology.*
SPCK	Society for Promoting Christian Knowledge.
SRO(B)	Suffolk Record Office (Bury St. Edmunds branch).
SRO(I)	Suffolk Record Office (Ipswich branch).

The Settlement, *pages 1–4*

1. E. Ekwall, *Oxford Dictionary of English Place Names* (1960), 222.
2. O. Rackham, *Ancient Woodland* (1980), 120.
3. Map of Hartest Farm, 1782: SRO(B), Acc 2225 (part).
   Hartest Tithe Map, 1839: SRO(B), T126/2.
4. Lease of Hartest Wood, 1729: SRO(B), HA519/608 (part).
5. Manorial Court presentment, 1712: SRO(B), HA519/605 (part).
6. S. H. A. Hervey, *Suffolk in 1327: subsidy return,* Suffolk Green Books, No. IX, Vol, II (1906), 143.

Agriculture, *pages 5–12*

1. J. Thirsk, *Agrarian History of England and Wales,* Vol. IV (1967), 41.
2. Robert Ryece's 'Breviary of Suffolk' in Lord Francis Hervey (ed.), *Suffolk in the XVIIth century* (1902), 26.
3. Robert Ryece, 30.
4. Terrier of Boxted Manor, 1630: SRO(B), HA519/11.
5. Probate inventory of Edward Browse, 1650: SRO(B), IC500/3/3/146.
6. Probate inventory of Robert Cronshaye, gentleman, 1665: SRO(B), IC500/3/9/211.
7. Probate inventory of William Underwood, clothier, 1678: NRO, INV.60B/47.
8. Probate inventory of Margaret Orbell, widow, 1705: SRO(B), IC500/3/32/80.
9. Will of Robert Frost, smith, 1574: SRO(B), IC500/1/33/18.
10. Will of Edmund Copping, yeoman, 1601: SRO(B), IC500/1/60/36.
11. Probate inventory of Ann Cranshaw, widow, 1703: SRO(B), IC500/3/30/7.
12. Probate inventory of John Frost, tanner, 1663: SRO(B), IC500/3/8/139.
13. Probate inventory of William Stearn, yeoman, 1678: SRO(B), IC500/3/19/221.
14. Probate inventory of Benjamine Lilly, wheelwright, 1667: SRO(B), IC500/3/11/139.
15. Probate inventory of Thomas Cranshay, 1700: SRO(B), IC500/3/27/58.
16. Probate inventory of William Shelly, 1703: SRO(B), IC500/3/20/27.
17. J. Thirsk, 47.
18. Probate inventory of Randal Lock, 1710: SRO(B), IC500/3/36/31.
19. Probate inventory of Thomas Cronshay, Rector, 1616: NRO, INV.27B/171.
20. Probate inventory of John Frost, tanner, 1663: SRO(B), IC500/3/8/139.
21. Probate inventory of Edward Johnson, gentleman, 1700: SRO(B), IC500/3/27/4.
22. Probate inventory of Ann Cranshaw, widow, 1703: SRO(B), IC500/3/30/7.

23. Will of Thomas Goshawk, yeoman, 1629: SRO(B), IC500/1/85/54.
24. Will of Richard Cronshay, 1685: SRO(B), IC500/1/139/27.
25. Will of James Hibble, 1569: SRO(B), IC500/1/33/128.
26. Probate inventory of Randal Lock, 1710: SRO(B), IC500/3/36/31.
27. Probate inventory of Robert Cranshay, 1664: SRO(B), IC500/3/9/211.
28. Probate inventory of Ann Cranshaw, widow, 1703: SRO(B), IC500/3/30/7.

Cloth Trade, *pages 13–16*

1. Robert Ryece, 23.
2. Will of John Frost, 1609: SRO(B), IC500/1/66/112.
3. Probate inventory of Thomas Underwood, singleman, 1661: SRO(B), IC500/3/5/189.
4. Probate inventory of William Underwood, clothier, 1678: NRO, INV.60B/47.
5. Probate inventory of Elizabeth Underwood, widow, 1678: NRO, INV.60B/57.
6. Probate inventory of James Jackson, stapler, 1678: SRO(B), IC500/3/19/184.
7. Will of William Bray, weaver, 1639: SRO(B), IC500/1/94/42.
8. Probate inventory of John Metcalf, woolcomber, 1707: SRO(B), IC500/3/34/1.
9. Probate inventory of James Jackson, yeoman, 1700: SRO(B), IC500/3/27/48.
10. Probate inventory of John Bonger, yeoman, 1701: SRO(B), IC500/3/28/69.
11. Probate inventory of William Shelly, 1703: SRO(B), IC500/3/30/27.

Population, *pages 17–18*

1. Hartest Parish Register: SRO(B), FL577/4/1.
2. C. H. E. White, 'The condition of the Archdeaconries of Sudbury and Suffolk', *PSIA,* XI (1903), 1–46.
3. E. A. Wrigley and R. S. Schofield, *The Population History of England, 1541–1871,* (1981).
4. Petition of the copyholders of Hartest, 1608: PRO, SP14/40/21.
5. Petition for a brief, 1651: SRO(B), FL577/5/2.
6. S. H. A. Hervey, *Suffolk in 1674, the Hearth Tax Returns,* Suffolk Green Books, No. XI, Vol. 13, (1905) 136.
7. D. P. Dymond, 'Suffolk and the Compton Census of 1676', in *Suffolk Review,* Vol. 3, (1966) 103–18.

The Church before the Reformation, *pages 19–20.*

1. Will of John Marlton, butcher, 1529: SRO(B), IC500/1/4/17.
2. SRO(B) IC500/2/12/26.
3. Will of John Phillipson, yeoman, 1546: SRO(B), IC500/2/21/656.
4. Will of William Hall, 1471: IC500/2/11/36.
5. Will of John Gardiner, 1519: IC500/2/14/28.
6. Will of John Mancer, curate of Shimpling, 1521: NRO, Alabaster 104.
7. Will of Thomas Gardiner, 1524: PRO, PCC, Bodfelde 24.
8. SRO(B) IC500/2/12/26.
9. Will of John Walkelyng, 1431: PRO, PCC, Luffenam 13.
10. Will of Robert Caston, 1494: SRO(B), IC500/2/13/22.
11. Will of Ralph Mason, 1496: SRO(B), IC500/2/13/35.
12. Will of John Mancer, curate of Shimpling, 1521: NRO, Alabaster 104.
13. Will of Rose Rand of Sudbury, 1535: SRO(B), IC500/1/6/2.

Civil War, *pages 21–24*

1. Clarendon, Earl, *History of the Rebellion and Civil Wars in England,* vol. 1 (1702 ed.) 412.
2. All quotations from, *Mercurius Rusticus,* The English Revolution III, Newsbooks, Oxford Royalist, vol. 4, 69–70.
3. House of Commons Journal, vol. 5, 684: HLRO.
4. A. G. Matthews, *Walker Revised,* (1948), 335.
5. Petition of Frederick Gibb, 1642: HLRO, Main Papers, 10 October 1642.
6. House of Commons Journal, vol. 5, 794: HLRO.
7. A. G. Matthews, 335.
8. Petition of Richard Duckworth 1660: PRO, Calendar of State Papers 1660, 216.
9. Lease of Place Farm, 1645: SRO(B), HA519/1048.
10. *East Anglian Notes and Queries,* New Series, vol. 10, 329. The original book from which this extract was taken is now lost.
11. C. H. E. White (ed.), *The Journal of William Dowsing 1643–4,* (1885), 6.
12. C. H. Firth and R. S. Rait, *Acts and Ordinances of the Interregnum 1642–60,* vol. 1, 425.

Death, *pages 25–30*

1. C. Creighton, *A History of Epidemics in Britain,* vol. 1. (1891), 506.
2. Will of Frances Reymond, 1637: SRO(B), IC500/1/92/124.
3. C. Creighton, 533, 541.
4. Will of William Bray, weaver, 1639: SRO(B), IC500/1/94/42.
5. Will of Thomas How, webster, 1639: SRO(B), IC500/1/121/10.
6. Will of Peter Borham, 1640: SRO(B), IC500/1/94/170.
7. Will of Alice Farrow, 1649: SRO(B), IC500/1/106/52.
8. Will of John Hibble, 1649: SRO(B), IC500/106/112.
9. Cockfield Parish Register: SRO(B), FL552/4/1.
10. Shimpling Parish Register: SRO(B), FL624/4/1.
11. Suffolk Quarter Sessions Minute Book: SRO(I), B105/2/7, fol. 24r.
12. Suffolk Quarter Sessions Minute Book: SRO (I), B105/2/7, fol. 32v.

The Grave, *pages 31–32*

1. Will of John Marlton, butcher, 1529: SRO(B), IC500/1/4/17.
2. Will of John Copyn, yeoman, 1531: SRO(B), IC500/2/19/95.
3. Will of Augustine How, singleman, 1691: SRO(B), IC500/1/150/93, and IC500/1/151/27.
4. Will of John Phillipson, yeoman, 1546: SRO(B), IC500/2/21/656.
5. Will of Ann Rokewood, singlewoman, 1572: SRO(B), IC500/1/31/78.
6. Will of William Hall, yeoman, 1608: SRO(B), IC500/1/66/63.
7. Will of Thomas Cronshay, Rector, 1615: NRO, Angell 135.

And Beyond the Grave, *pages 33–34*

1. Will of Katherine Frost, 1539: SRO(B), IC500/1/4/106b.
2. Will of Edmund Jonson, yeoman, 1506: SRO(B), IC500/1/27/151.
3. Will of Robert Peele, 1573: SRO(B), IC500/1/32/116.
4. M. Spufford, *Contrasting Communities,* (1974), 320ff.

5. Will of John Copping, yeoman, 1506: SRO(B), IC500/2/13/146.
6. Will of Joan Everyde, widow, 1543: SRO(B), IC500/2/19/452.
7. Will of James Frost, husbandman, 1551: SRO(B), IC500/1/11/18.
8. Will of John Heble, 1559: SRO(B), IC500/1/3/148.
9. Will of William Mayhew, 1575: SRO(B), IC500/1/34/63.
10. Will of Robert Frost, smyth, 1574: SRO(B), IC500/1/33/18.
11. Will of Thomas Wright, gentleman, 1646: SRO(B), IC500/1/105/75.
12. Will of Robert Enas, say weaver, 1684: SRO(B), IC500/1/139/24.
13. Will of Thomas Cronshay, gentleman, 1698: SRO(B), IC500/1/154/64.

The Fall of the Church Tower, *pages 35–38*

1. Petition for a brief, 1651: SRO(B), FL577/5/2.
2. The method used in this calculation was to multiply the number of families by 4.3 and 4.5. This, however, results in an over estimate of between 100 and 150 people.
3. Contract with Thomas Moore to rebuild the tower, 1652: SRO(B), HA519/590.
4. Receipt of Thomas Moore, 1652: SRO(B), HA519/591.
5. Accounts of Thomas Moore, 1652: SRO(B), HA519/592 and 593.

Charities, *pages 39–42*

1. The details of the endowments are taken from *The Charities in the County of Suffolk* (1828–40).
2. Will of Thomas Wright, gentleman, 1646: SRO(B), IC500/1/105/75.
3. Will of Thomas Sparke of Rougham, gentleman, 1721: SRO(B), IC500/1/178/60.
4. Will of Katherine Frost, 1539: SRO(B), IC500/1/4/106b.
5. Will of Thomasyn Phillipson, 1570: SRO(B), IC500/1/30/27.
6. Will of John Hayward, 1607: SRO(B), IC500/1/66/43.
7. Will of Thomas Underwood, yeoman, 1629: SRO(B), IC500/1/87/140.
8. Will of John Hall, yeoman, 1628: SRO(B), IC500/1/85/97.
9. Will of Richard Cranshay, 1685: SRO(B), IC500/1/139/27.
10. Will of George Hibble, yeoman, 1695: SRO(B), IC500/1/149/80.

Boxted Tithe Agreement, *pages 43–45*

1. Statement by John Pawsey and Elizabeth Gault, 1682: SRO(B), HA519/585(b).

Philippa Munnings: The Hartest Witch?, *page 47*

1. F. Hutchinson, *An Historical Essay Concerning Witchcraft,* (1718), 59–60.
2. C. L. Ewen, *Witchcraft and Demonianism,* (1933), 373.
3. F. Hutchinson, 59.
4. Hartest Parish Register: SRO(B), FL577/4/2.

John Frost: The Tanner, *pages 47–48*

1. Probate inventory of John Frost, tanner, 1663: SRO(B), IC500/3/8/139; his Will, 1661: SRO(B), IC500/1/115/113.

Two Hartest Shopkeepers, *pages 49–56*

1. Will of Andrew Byatt, 'gentleman', 1666: SRO(B), IC500/1/122/104.
2. Probate inventory of Andrew Byatt, 'grocer', 1670: SRO(B), IC500/3/15/190.
3. Probate inventory of Thomas Orbell, grocer, 1720: SRO(B), IC500/3/43/31.

The Weller Poley Family, *pages 57–65*

1. Grant of Boxted Hall, 1561: SRO(B), HA519/24.
2. Declaration by Sir John Poley, 1636: SRO(B), HA519/25.
3. N. Pevsner, *The Buildings of England: Suffolk,* (1974), 106. John Bushnell, sculptor, died 1701. He was eccentric and died insane, could this be the real reason for the frog earring?
4. Notes on the frog earring: SRO(B), HA519/201/1–5.
5. Sir John Cullum's Church Notes: SRO(B), E2/33/17.1, p. 248.
6. Terrier of Boxted Hall, 1630: SRO(B), HA519/11.
7. Will of Sir William Poley, 1658: SRO(B), HA519/409.
8. Boxted Parish Register: SRO(B), FL530/1/1.
9. Boxted Overseers accounts: SRO(B), FL530/1/1.
10. Will of John Poley, 1757: SRO(B), HA519/794.
11. Letter from James Nelthorpe, 1757: SRO(B), HA519/204.
12. Letter from William Crofts, 1767: SRO(B), HA519/189.
13. *Return of the owners of land in 1873,* vol. II, Suffolk section, (1875), 32.
14. Farrer Collection, Boxted: SRO(B), HD526/17/7.

The Cronshay Family of 'Kings', *pages 66–73*

1. Will of Thomas Cronshay, Rector, 1615: NRO, Angell 135.
2. Probate inventory of Thomas Cronshay, Rector, 1616: NRO, 27B/171.
3. Our thanks are due to Sylvia Colman for her help with the reconstruction.
4. Will of Robert Cronshay, gentleman, 1664: SRO(B), IC500/1/116/179.
5. Probate inventory of Robert Cronshay, gentleman, 1664: SRO(B), IC500/3/9/211.
6. Probate inventory of Robert Cronshay, 1692: SRCO(B), IC500/3/24/42.
7. Probate inventory of Thomas Cronshay, 1700: SRO(B), IC500/3/27/58.
8. Sale of 'Kings' to Thomas Sargent, 1711: SRO(B), HA519/573.

The Underwood Family, *pages 74–78*

1. Will of Thomas Underwood, yeoman, 1631: SRO(B), IC500/1/87/140.
2. Will of Thomas Underwood, yeoman, 1651: SRO(B), IC500/1/108/85.
3. Lease of 'Sorrells', 1788: SRO(B), HA519/679.
4. Lease of Cook's Farm, 1624: SRO(B), HA519/467 and 472.
5. Probate inventory of Thomas Underwood, yeoman, 1652: SRO(B), HA519/435.
6. Will of John Underwood, yeoman, 1669: SRO(B), IC500/1/121/95.
7. Probate inventory of John Underwood, yeoman, 1669: SRO(B), IC500/3/14/70.
8. Will of William Underwood, clothier, 1678: NRO, OW.1678, No. 56.
9. Will of Elizabeth Underwood, widow, 1678: NRO, OW.1678, No. 57.

The Manor of Hartest Hall, *pages 79–82*

1. Will of Thomas Cronshay, Rector, 1615: NRO, Angell 135.

2. Petition of the copyholders of Hartest, 1608: PRO, SP14/40/21.
3. Manorial customs of 1644–56, copied in 1765: SRO(B), HA519/83.
4. Glebe Terrier, 1638: SRO(B), E4/4/3.
5. Will of William Bridge, yeoman, 1597: SRO(B), IC500/1/55/52.
6. Document in the Crown Inn.
7. David Davey, 'A Journal of Excursions Through the County of Suffolk' (1823–1844); J. Blatchly (ed.) *Suffolk Record Society,* Vol. 24 (1982), 174.

Hartest in 1839, *page 83*

1. Hartest Tithe Map 1839: SRO(B), T126/182.
2. Census Returns, 1841: SRO(B), J578/1.

The Restoration of the Church 1879–80, *page 101–102*

1. Hartest Vestry Book: SRO(B), FL577/5/1.
2. Faculty application, 1879: SRO(B), FE500/6/2.
3. David Davy's Church Notes: SRO(B), 2426/1 (Microfilm of Add. Mss. 19077–8).
4. Bury and Norwich Post, 20 June 1859.

The Congregationalists, *pages 103–105*

1. V. B. Redstone, *Records of Protestant Dissenters in Suffolk,* (1912), 35.
2. Stansfield Congregational Church Book: SRO(B), FK3/506/1.
3. Hartest Congregational Church Book: SRO(B), FK3/503/1.
4. Hartest Church Book, 4.
5. Hartest Church Book, 42.
6. Hartest Church Book, 43.

The Plymouth Brethren, *pages 107–108.*

1. W. A. Copinger, *Suffolk Records,* (1904), vol. 3, 89.

The Rectory, *page 111*

1. Glebe Terrier, 1613: SRO(B), E14/4/1.
2. Glebe Terrier, 1638: SRO(B), E14/4/3.
3. Faculty application, 1821: SRO(B), 806/2/9.

Schools in Hartest, *pages 115–117*

1. Will of Alice Gardiner, 1567: SRO(B), IC500/1/19/108.
2. SPCK Abstract Letter Book, 1/1456.
3. SPCK Abstract Letter Books, 2/2087 and 2/2217.
4. Hartest Parish Register: SRO(B), FL577/4/3.
5. Will of Thomas Sparkes of Rougham, gentleman, 1721: SRO(B), IC500/1/178/60.
6. Sparke's Charity Minute Book: SRO(B), GB508/1.
7. Report of the Select Committee on the Education of the Poor, 1818.
8. Abstract of Education Returns, 1833.

Extracts from Hartest School Log Book, *pages 118–127*

1. Log Book: SRO(B), 2199/1/3.

Postal Services, *pages 130–131*

1. Report by Graham Hart to Francis Freeling, 1826: POA, Post 40/324/302.
2. Petition of Robert Gill, 1827: POA, Post 40/337/10.
3. Letter from Thomas Hallifax of Chadacre to Sir Francis Freeling, 1831: POA, 40/517/563.

Queen Victoria's Jubilee Celebrations, *page 133*

1. Bury and Norwich Post, 28 June 1887.
2. Bury and Norwich Post, 29 June 1897.

Hartest Fair, *page 135*

1. Bury and Norwich Post, 12 July 1859.

Hartest Stone, *page 137*

1. Bury and Norwich Post, 12 July 1859.

Letters from Rev. Arthur Packer to John Weller Poley, *pages 139–140*

1. Letters: SRO(B), HA519/2157–2163.

General Index

Index of Contemporary Names

A person's place of residence is Hartest, unless otherwise stated.

ISBN 0 9510180 0 0